JUST *one* HOUR

A Practical Guide to
Effective Bible Study

REV. DR. WINELLE KIRTON-ROBERTS

authorHOUSE®

AuthorHouse™
1663 Liberty Drive
Bloomington, IN 47403
www.authorhouse.com
Phone: 833-262-8899

Published by AuthorHouse 06/07/2022

ISBN: 978-1-6655-5933-1 (sc)
ISBN: 978-1-6655-5934-8 (e)

Library of Congress Control Number: 2022908674

Print information available on the last page.

This book is printed on acid-free paper.

CONTENTS

CONTENTS

INTRODUCTION: WHY THIS BOOK?

In 1992, I was on my summer assignment at the Lebanon/Newfield (Enon) congregations, Antigua Conference. At the time, the Lebanon congregation had introduced a Sunday evening Bible study with the hope of gaining greater interest and increasing the attendance at Bible study. One of my assignments was to conduct this Bible study for July and August. While I had led Bible studies in previous student assignments, this was the first time that I was responsible for an entire series.

I was both excited and anxious at the same time. And, after much prayer, study, and reflection, I drafted a handwritten Bible study schedule on the book of Colossians. This schedule included the date, the topic, and the scripture reading.

I waited with much trepidation on that first Bible study evening, wondering whether members would respond positively to the pastor's appeal to attend. And, if they came, would they be inspired enough to continue attending for the summer? As predicted by the pastor, a faithful few turned out that first evening. However, we had such an insightful and stimulating study that the interest and attendance increased every week. Most importantly, members testified that they grew spiritually, and that, for them, the Bible was not just a book to read on Sundays but God's inspired Word for personal growth.

I learned five important lessons from that first Bible study series:

1. Bible study is an effective evangelistic tool in challenging members to a commitment to faith in Jesus Christ.

2. Bible study is a powerful Christian education tool in helping believers to mature in the Christian faith.
3. Bible study is meaningful when careful attention is given to the preparation and presentation.
4. Bible study fosters Christian fellowship, which strengthens pastoral relationships.
5. Bible study greatly contributes to the spiritual growth of the pastor/Christian leader.

Since then, planning and teaching series of Bible studies has been my pastoral passion that has spanned my three calls. This began with the most intimate yet enthusiastic discussions at Chaguanas, Trinidad, my first congregation. In Barbados, it continued with the thought-provoking, stirring and spirited sessions at Calvary, Barbados. At the sister congregation, Grace Hill, I had the most unique experience. With confirmation classes scheduled just before Bible study, I encouraged the youth to stay on for the hour of Bible study. As a result, we had the most energetic, engaging, and memorable intergenerational Bible studies.

Bible study at Memorial, St. Thomas, Virgin Islands, was the highlight of my ministry. The depth of the studies, the robust discussions, and the joyful fellowship resulted in members' unswerving commitment to the study of the Word. Not only were church officers and members faithful in attendance, but the study also attracted members of the community. As pastor, I looked forward every Wednesday to Bible study because I never knew what would happen—what new insight someone would share, what question would stump me, and what joke would make my heart merry.

After twenty-nine years of pastoral ministry, I have concluded that the strength and vibrancy of the church's Bible study is a key determinant of the spiritual health and well-being of the church. Even if the Sunday morning worship is lively, with great singing and anointed preaching, we will remain babes in Christ, waiting for the next bottle of milk for gratification, if we are not studying the Bible.

There is no wonder that it had been the practice of the Moravian churches to divide the church into small "choirs," or classes, so that they could get deeper in the Word of God. This was the place where they searched the scriptures and applied them to their lives. Since these choirs have ceased to exist, the Bible study has become the place for the solid food of God's Word.

Bible study is the foundation for discipleship and should be the highlight of every congregation. I have written this book, *Just One Hour*, for three reasons:

1. **To keep a promise**

Over the years, members and visitors alike would ask me for Bible study notes, especially if they missed a class. Also, Christian leaders and pastors who had heard of the specific series would request my script. While I was always willing to loan copies of the books I used in preparing the series, I never felt comfortable in giving my personal notes. This was largely because of the typographical and grammatical errors and more so because of corrections I would have to make to the Bible references. At the end of every series, I would commit myself to revising the study so that it could be a ministry to someone. This book is the fulfilment of my promises to the requests for my studies.

2. **As a resource for personal study**

This book can be used as a resource to develop the believer's personal faith in Christ. It is not a replacement for weekly Bible study, but it can be used as a tool for family devotions. Further, the study can be used in small settings, like fellowships, groups, or ministries in the church. As an outreach in the workplace or community, the study is a helpful guide to build or foster a Christian group. The studies are outlined in such a way that each series can be spread over weeks or even months. There are at least five years of Bible study in this book!

3. **As a handbook for pastors and Christian leaders**

Pastors and Christian leaders are often thinking of what to do for their next Bible study series. This book contains Bible study material that can be used verbatim or as a supplement to other resources for the weekly Bible study. Like all other study guides, the book will not eliminate the need for personal reflection, research, and study. This will help the pastor/Christian leader to add other Bible references and to make the necessary changes for contextual relevance.

PART 1

Principles and Plans

CHAPTER 1

The Word of God in The Bible

> The Spirit alone gives eternal life.
> Human effort accomplishes nothing.
> And the very words I have spoken
> to you are spirit and life.
> —John 6:63

On the shelves of bookstores, libraries, and airport newsstands are hundreds of inspirational best-selling books. Christian and non-Christian authors have become millionaires by writing books that have motivated readers to improve their lives, make positive changes, and find purpose and peace in life. *Be the Best You, Seven Habits of an Effective Leader, The Secret to Happiness, How to Eat Right, Think and Grow Rich, Chicken Soup for the Soul,* and *Releasing the Power of God in You* are but some of the titles of these motivational books. If you are like me, you cannot resist buying these books in the hope that they might tell you something you don't already know.

Commendably, these authors advocate for good habits, challenge mediocrity, and support maximizing one's potential. Ultimately, the principle behind all of the themes is a change in one's thinking, attitude, and behavior. Some who faithfully adhere to the recommendations do conquer failure and fear and are set on a path to purposeful living.

Yet even by the authors' admissions, the books are limited in scope. And while a temporary change is evident, there is no long-term transformation.

But there is a book whose authors were inspired by God and that contains not just self-help instructions or stories of inspiration but the life-giving Word of God. This book is for the whole person—mind, body, and soul. It attends to all our human needs. It inspires, motivates, instructs, and—most importantly—gives life

The Bible

The Bible is also referred to as the Holy Book, the Holy Scriptures, or the Good Book. The word *bible* derives from the Greek word *biblion,* which means "book." Attributed to about forty authors, the Bible is the *logos,* or the written God.

Around two hundred years after the coming of Jesus Christ, these written texts were authorized as a canon of sacred scriptures. The canonical Bible was divided into the thirty-seven books of the Old Testament and the twenty-nine books of the New Testament. Some other books, regarded as of unknown origin, did not make it into the canon; these are referred to as the Apocrypha. The Roman Catholic and Orthodox traditions do include some of these as sacred readings, but the Protestants do not.

The Bible, as we know it, was not written in a chronological order. The first book believed to have been written is Job, more than 3,400 years ago. The Revelation of John was written about 1,900 years ago and is the most recent book to have been written. Most Bible scholars agree that Mark was the first Gospel to be written, followed by Luke, Matthew, and John. The order, therefore, is not as important as the content of the message. It is the interpretation and application of the Word of God to the life of the people of God. This is the *rhema,* or spoken word. The spoken word always confirms the written word.

> And Mary said, "Behold, I am the servant of the Lord; let it be to me according to your word." And the angel departed from her. (Luke 1:38)

In the canonical Bible, one finds the laws of God, history, prophesies, poetry, romance, the life and teachings of Jesus Christ, letters of the apostles, and the final revelation. The Bible is still the most-read book in the world. From the historian who is searching for facts, to the religious critic who is looking for contradictions; from the Bible scholars who are obsessed with inaccuracies of the text, to the devout believer for whom it is daily bread, the Bible has never lost its appeal.

One may get out of the Bible what one is searching for. The purpose of the written Word of God is not to be lost in the quest for knowledge and understanding. Through a personal faith and reverence for God, one receives the life-giving God: "The fear of the

LORD is the beginning of wisdom, and knowledge of the Holy One is understanding" (Proverbs 9:10 NLT).

❖ Versions and Translations

The Bible was written in three original languages: Hebrew, Aramaic, and Greek. The Old Testament was generally written in Hebrew, while the New Testament and the books of Daniel and Ezra were written in Aramaic. As Christianity spread and the original languages became unknown, translations became necessary. Over the centuries, the Bible was translated into various languages so that the followers of Christ could read the scriptures. Several early church leaders, including John Huss, devoted their lives to translating the Bible into a new language. The first English translation was done in the late fourteenth century.

Christians have been most familiar with the King James Version, which was published in 1611. This was close to three hundred years after the first English translation of the Bible. The Authorized version, as it is called, was edited by forty-seven scholars who were commissioned by King James. The Church of England needed a Bible for religious but also political reasons. The King James Version of the Bible has been held dear by many up to this day. There are some who refuse to accept other versions of the Bible.

Since language changes, the earlier versions of the Bible, including the KJV, are often revised to meet current needs. When a translation is edited, it is known as a new "version" of the Bible. However, when a scholar returns to the original languages and works directly with the source text to translate it into contemporary words, the result is referred to as a translation. For example, compare the New International Version of the Bible to the New Living Translation.

Today, there is a wide variety of versions, translations, and revisions of the Bible. There is no perfect version or translation; personal preference may serve as a guide. The general objective is to provide the written Word in a format that is as comprehensible as possible, while maintaining the original meaning. The Amplified Version, for instance, includes several words and phrases to interpret one original word. One popular paraphrasing of the Bible is called *The Message* by Eugene Petersen.

Consider the following versions and translations of the well-known text John 3:16.

> **KJV**: For God so loved the world that he gave His only begotten Son that whosoever believeth in him should not perish but have everlasting life.

> **NIV**: For God so loved the world that he gave his one and only Son, that whoever believes in him shall not perish but have eternal life.

NLT: For this is how God loved the world: He gave his one and only Son, so that everyone who believes in him will not perish but have eternal life.

Amplified: For God so [greatly] loved and dearly prized the world, that He [even] gave His [One and] only begotten Son, so that whoever believes and trusts in Him [as Savior] shall not perish, but have eternal life.

Message Bible: This is how much God loved the world. He gave his son, his one and only son. And this why: so that no need to be destroyed; by believing in him, anyone can have a whole and lasting life.

Today, as the gospel is preached to many nations, there are still more translations in native languages.

Christians should choose a version or translation that they can most understand and that helps them to apply the scriptures to their lives. I have often recommended the New Living Translation, which has kept its use of words as close to the original language as possible and yet is readily understood.

❖ Study Bibles

Study Bibles were first published for seminarians and serious lay students of the Bible. In general, study Bibles include cross-references of texts, context of the book and chapter, Hebrew or Greek terms, biblical maps, and abbreviated commentaries. This additional information is not only helpful in preparing to present the spoken Word but in maturing in the faith.

There are also three primary accompaniments to the study Bible: concordance, commentary, and lexicon. A concordance provides references throughout the Bible to each in a list of terms. For example, one can use a concordance to find all references to the word *faith*. As a summer student at Memorial, I was given a "strong exhaustive concordance" by a faithful member. A commentary provides historic background and often gives the meaning of the original words. One of the best-known commentaries is by Matthew Henry. Serious students also use the Hebrew or Greek lexicons. Through these sources, you have the translations of the original language. Maps can be purchased separately to study the geographical locations named in the Bible and how these sites have evolved over the years.

Just as there are versions and translations of the Bible, there are several concordances, commentaries, and lexicons. Today, most of these are online, although one must be careful the source of information. As a study Bible for personal growth, I recommend the Life

Application Study Bible. It comes in most versions of the Bible and is comprehensive for the student of the Bible.

❖ From Scrolls to Smartphones

The earliest writings of the sacred texts were on scrolls, made from either papyrus (plant-based) or parchment (animal-based). In the earlier versions, the texts were written on separate sheets, but just before the coming of Jesus Christ, these were stitched together and resembled a modern book. They were kept in the temple. Jesus read from one of these scrolls, as recorded in Luke 4:17:

> The scroll of Isaiah the prophet was handed to him. He unrolled the scroll and found the place where this was written.

The scribes were responsible for writing, interpreting, and preserving the scrolls. They played a key role among the people of God. Ezra is an example.

> This Ezra was a scribe who was well versed in the Law of Moses, which the LORD, the God of Israel, had given to the people of Israel. He came up to Jerusalem from Babylon, and the king gave him everything he asked for, because the gracious hand of the LORD his God was on him. (Ezra 7:6)

As protectors of the written texts, the scribes eventually became very self-righteous and arrogant. Jesus showed little tolerance for this behavior.

> And so, you cancel the word of God in order to hand down your own tradition. And this is only one example among many others. (Mark 7:13)

As late as 1947, sacred texts were found in hundreds of caves in the Qumran area; these are the Dead Sea Scrolls. For centuries, the sacred texts were kept in the temple.

It is hard to believe that the great Reformers like John Huss and Martin Luther fought to have every believer read the Bible for themselves. Even so, it was only in recent decades that personal copies of the Bible became more common. Today, many homes have several copies of the Bible. Most revolutionary, however, is the Bible available at your fingertips—the current generation is more likely to read the Bible from their tablets or smartphones.

If you are disciplined enough to pull out your smartphone or tablet and read the scripture without being distracted by WhatsApp, Facebook, or Instagram, then use the technology. If you find that you spend an hour reading and responding to messages, compared with five minutes reading the scripture, it may be a good idea to reserve the mobile device for travel. It is not old-fashioned by any means to read a printed Bible.

❖ **Study**

Like all literature, it is one thing to read the Bible and another to understand it. Christian missionaries devoted themselves to helping converts learn to read so that they could read the Bible. Yet a proof of one's knowledge of scripture was based on whether one could memorize Bible chapters and verses. Unfortunately, while followers were able to repeat scripture, they were not always able to explain it. This was because they did not understand.

The Ethiopian eunuch in Acts 8:26–40 could have read Isaiah, but when he was asked if he understood it, he replied, "How can I, unless someone instructs me?"

From the scripture, the eunuch asked questions that Philip answered. This time of instruction resulted in the eunuch's public confession of faith.

It is not enough for us to read; we need to have instruction and discussion on the text. Reading and meditating on the scriptures daily is important, but it is in the context of Bible study that we become enlightened on the text, ask questions, and are guided by someone who has devoted time to the study of the Word.

> Study to shew thyself approved unto God, a workman that needeth not
> to be ashamed, rightly dividing the word of truth. (2 Timothy 2:15 KJV)

CHAPTER 2

What Bible Study is Not

> Knowing this first, that no prophecy of the
> scripture is of any private interpretation. For
> the prophecy came not in old time by the
> will of man: but holy men of God spake as
> they were moved by the Holy Ghost.
> —2 Peter 1:20–21

Whether a gathering of three faithful souls or a robust group of sixty members, every church should have Bible study. This is a time devoted to instruction in the Word of God. To be effective, this designated time should be focused on God's Word, for it is possible for Bible studies to be something other than study.

Therefore, Bible study is not:

❖ Prayer Meeting

Prayer is very important for the church. It is the heartbeat of the Christian life. It is a time to adore our God, confess our sins, give thanks, and make intercessions for all. In the time of the apostles, the followers of Christ gave attention to various aspects of the ministry of the church. According to Acts 2:42, teaching was at the top of the list:

All the believers devoted themselves to the apostles' teaching, and to fellowship and to sharing in meals (including the Lord's Supper) and to prayer.

The public ministry, then, was teaching, public worship, Holy Communion, and prayer meeting, all of which have a place in the advancement of the kingdom of God. The weekly prayer meeting should be given its due focus and be separated from the Bible study. Even if, for practical reasons, the two are on held on the same day, it should be clear which part is dedicated to the study of the Word. Some may choose to begin or end the Bible study with special prayer requests, along with either a closing or opening prayer. This is not to say that the pastor/leader should not be being sensitive to the Spirit of God, for there will be times of crisis and need when the prepared Bible study may have to be set aside for a time of prayer. But to have Bible study as a time of prayer is to take away from the power of equipping the saints for the work of ministry.

❖ **Song Service**

As Christians, we like to sing. As we are led by the Spirit of God, we respond by singing our praises unto God.

> Don't be drunk with wine, because that will ruin your life. Instead be filled with the Holy Spirit, singing Psalms and Hymns and spiritual songs among yourselves, and making music to the Lord in your Lord. (Ephesians 5:18–19)

If we leave it up to believers, they would sing, and sing, and sing, but when it comes to the proclamation of the Word, they tune out. While singing lifts our spirits and encourages us, it is the Word of God that sustains. Using the Bible study as a time for singing will help the believer for that moment.

When Jesus was tempted by Satan in the wilderness, Jesus spoke the Word of God. He knew and had memorized the Word. Making Bible study a time for singing, whether hymns, sacred songs, or contemporary worship, robs believers of the opportunity for rooting their faith. Study of the Word moves beyond the emotions and helps believers to have that Word as a sword for life.

> Thy word have I hid in my heart so that I might not sin against thee. (Psalm 119:11)

❖ Midweek Service

Some churches have found that members are more likely to come to a midweek service than attend a Bible study. Many believers may not have confidence in their own reading and are often afraid of being called upon to read. Others are more comfortable being an inactive participant than an active one. It is interesting to observe that while the Lenten services run at the same time as Bible study in the churches, they are much better attended. An Ash Wednesday service can have attendance close to a Sunday morning service. The midweek service takes the format of a shortened version of the Sunday morning worship, with a time of praise, testimony, and preaching. This is better received by the members, and for pastors/leaders, it may be easier to expound on a single scripture than to take the time to provide references that are needed for a Bible study. Midweek services have their place, and some churches might be able to accommodate both. Since during a sermon is not usually a good time to ask questions, it is not healthy for the growth of members to sit and listen to someone again.

❖ Seminary Class

There is a lot to learn from the Bible. In seminary or Bible college, classes provide that depth. While we want our doctors to explain our health in as detailed a form as possible, it is not necessary for us to know all the technical terms, which can be baffling and confusing. Similarly, to use Bible study as a time to present all the jargon of scripture will not necessarily build anyone's faith. Knowledge of Greek and Hebrew can help one to understand the scripture and have a better understanding of the Word. Further, knowing more of the historic background or even the writing of scripture can be good. Bible study, however, is not the time to engage in all the translations of verbs.

> Don't let anyone capture you with empty philosophies and high-sounding nonsense that come from human thinking and from the spiritual powers of this world rather than from Christ. (Colossians 2:8)

The balance of providing information is very important, but it is not to be a full debate.

❖ Group Therapy

Every day, we battle with various issues and struggles in life. A fellowship of Christians is often a safe space to share what one is personally going through.

Bear ye one another's burdens and so fulfil the law of Christ. (Galatians 6:2)

As the scriptures are read, they have a discerning impact and can lead to confession and testimony. Room must be made in Bible study for that level of personal sharing. Because such sharing can be personally meaningful, it is possible to have that as a Bible study focus.

If a pastor or leader discerns that there is a need for follow-up on matters raised, then he/she should reach out for further pastoral care. One then must be careful that the Bible is not just a group therapy session. While scripture read will evoke a personal testimony or struggle, it is not the time of week to focus on individual battles. However, there are times when the silence should be broken. For example, I have had studies on suicide as members address issues of close loved ones who have attempted or succumbed to it.

But it is also possible for leaders, due to lack of preparation, to provoke emotions. Bible study is not only about sharing or unburdening but feeding of the Word of God in the lives of others.

❖ Political Forum

One professor encouraged pastors to have the Bible in one hand and the newspaper in the other. This is very important for the minister of the gospel—to keep in touch with reality. The most recent news item similarly can make for interesting discussion. Bible study can easily become a public debate. Jesus reminded us that we live in this world and should know what is happening.

> I am not asking that you take them out of the world, but that you keep
> them from the evil one. (John 17:15)

People share different sides of political parties and so on. While the church must not run from addressing important issues of climate change, immigration, gender equity, etc., it is not to consume the Bible study on an ongoing basis. Some leaders can be so in touch that they focus on political issues and not on the Bible.

I recall a church in Barbados that held a lunchtime forum to address current matters. This is the way to go. Occasional lectures or inviting public personalities to speak is always a good thing. It suggests that the church is not out of touch. But take care with discussion; it should not include Bible study.

❖ Bible Study Is Exegesis, Not "*I*"-*xegesis*

Biblical scholars define *exegesis* as an interpretation of the text or a critical explanation of it. The discipline of exegesis is to let the scripture speak for itself. That is, as you examine the text, you will find the application. Instead of *exegesis* we are sometimes guilty of I'*xegesis*. This is a coined word that is used to speak to reading your thoughts into the text. So, you begin with your situation and then try to find scripture to support it.

Bible study is not the place for 'I'*xegesis* but for the Christian who has the desire to let the Bible speak to him and her. One will find that in exegesis, there is a deep revelation that builds your faith and establishes your relationship with Jesus Christ.

Let Bible study be Bible study.

CHAPTER 3

Bible Study in One Hour

> Every scripture is inspired by God and useful
> for teaching, for reproof, for correction,
> and for training in righteousness, that the
> person dedicated to God may be capable
> and equipped for every good work.
> —2 Timothy 3:16–17

❖ Quench Not the Spirit

In a recently formed nondenominational church, the average length of the service on Sunday morning averaged around four hours. The worshippers often left around 1:00 p.m. after a 9:00 a.m. start of the service. The charismatic pastor would remind followers that they should not quench the Spirit of God. Therefore, there should be no limit to time in the house of God, as the unbelievers committed more hours to sports and others forms of entertainment.

One of the members, realizing that he was physically and emotionally wary of the time the Word was preached, chose to arrive at church close to the time that the pastor usually was ministering the Word of God. As he approached the service one Sunday morning, he was surprised to see that the church parking lot was empty. Thinking that he did not get an announcement about changes, he contacted a member, who informed him that the service was already over. The pastor had a flight that day to take one of his children to college, and he shortened the service so that he could get to the airport. The stunned member pondered and then asked, "If the church time is adjusted to meet the needs of the pastor and his family, shouldn't we be generally more considerate of the needs of all the families in the church? Is the Spirit quenched only when it does not have anything to do with the pastor?"

Sunday morning worship services have gradually extended in length over the years. The first thought might be that it's due to the length of sermons. To some extent, this is true, as the average sermon is over thirty minutes. To enhance the time of worship, however, one finds ministries in dance, song, drama, time of praise, etc. The average Sunday morning worship is just under two hours. The result is that Sunday evening services either are canceled or have low attendance.

There have been some recent changes, however, even in the nondenominational churches. A respect for time and the realization that worship is not confined to a public activity has resulted in many services being one hour, with an increase in attendance.

Like Sunday services, Bible studies can also be extended into the late evening, taking members and pastors away from their families. Like the Sunday worship, it is also important to examine our stewardship of time.

The average Bible study attendance is less than 10 percent of the Sunday worship attendance. That means that a small percentage of membership is going in depth in the Word, and this must be a concern for the church. I believe that when Bible study is the focus of what it ought to be, then in just one hour one can be effective.

❖ Time Is Everything

Churches are always assessing the timing of their Bible studies to find the most conducive times to reach as many members as possible. In many metropolitan cities, with members residing a far distance from the church, Bible studies have move to Sunday mornings, before or after the public worship. Some churches and ministries have chosen to set up online Bible studies, where you can stay in the comfort of your home and study the Word of God.

The traditional Wednesday evening Bible study at 7:30 p.m. may still work in some contexts, but it has increasingly become unpopular with the change of demographics and family structures. When I attended my first Bible study at Calvary, Barbados, in 1997, there were four faithful members. The study started at 7:30 p.m. I was waiting for others to arrive when one of the sisters said to me, "Rev! We are four and no more! Please start!" She further explained that that 7:30 was the best time for her, as it gave her enough time to complete an after-school activity before she came to the study. To her thinking, the members did not like Bible, and that's why they didn't come to Bible study.

Upon reflection and evaluation, I realized that the 7:30 time was fine when most members lived in the city or its environs. But that had changed. And with the rising criminal activity at night, most would rather be home than in the city.

With the support of the board, we decided to try to have a prayer meeting from 5:30 to 6:00 p.m. and have Bible study from 6:00 to 7:00 p.m. This appealed to younger families who came from work with their children. Interestingly enough, the children had their own fellowship. And to our surprise, more of the retired seniors attended because they preferred to get home by 7:30 p.m., rather than begin at that time. But even more astonishing was the attendance of men who said that they liked knowing there was a starting time and a finishing time.

Every context is different. It would be wise for the leadership of the church to investigate the best time to involve as many persons as possible.

Similarly, the pastors should create a Bible study schedule. Some churches have Bible study all year around, except in inclement weather. It is worth considering preparing schedules with a break of at least one month during the summer and two weeks around the Christmas. A break from Bible study is not necessarily a break from reading the Bible. Each pastor must be wise and sensitive.

Timing is very critical for effective Bible study. The day of the week, the time of the day, and the time of the year must be considered in planning.

> For everything there is a season, a time for every activity under heaven. (Ecclesiastes 3:1)

❖ Beyond the Gift of Teaching

There are teachers, and there are teachers. There are teachers who are qualified, trained, experienced, and knowledgeable but who are unable to inspire or motivate others to learn and succeed. Others are equally or sometimes less equipped but have the wherewithal to bring out the best in their students. One would say that the latter is a gift.

The Bible is clear that teaching is a spiritual gift.

> In his grace, God has given us different gifts for doing certain things well …
> if you are a teacher, teach well. (Romans 12:6a–7b)

Within the body of Christ, there are pastors and leaders who have the gift of teaching. God has given them the anointing, just as others are gifted evangelists, prophets, etc. However, the one biblical mandate of Jesus to his disciples was to teach.

Teach these new disciples to obey all the command I am giving you. And be sure of this: I am with you always even to the end of the age. (Matthew 28:20)

Theological colleges and seminaries usually have several classes on homiletics (preaching) but rarely have a class on teaching Bible study. Yet even with the anointed gift, the skills of teaching the Bible would help every leader. Some general skills may be found in Christian education.

When I was doing my master's in theology at Princeton Seminary, New Jersey, my supervisor recommended that I do the course "Teaching the Bible to Adults." It was an extra course that I didn't need to fulfil my credit requirements, but it was the most useful and practical course that I took.

To be an effective Bible study teacher, one must do the following:

Be prepared. You cannot prepare for Bible study half an hour before Bible study. It will show. Rather, prepare weeks ahead. You should know what you are studying and should read the scriptures. Use all the resources available to you.

Be prayerful. The time of Bible study should be committed to prayer—that is a given. It is a time of worship, and the presence of the Holy Spirit leads us aright.

Provide material. Some pastors prefer to order study books for members. Others choose to copy their material. I like to write on the board so that members can write in their notebooks. When you write, you committed more to memory.

Allow for discussion. Asking questions of members will be helpful for discussion and also will encourage members to ask questions or make comments. It is not a sermon to be preached. Discuss.

Be on time. Beginning on time is very important. It reflects the seriousness of the Bible study. This also means that you ensure that the space used for the study is ready, whether it is the sanctuary or a fellowship hall (which is preferable for writing).

Teaching is a Christian obligation to pass on the faith of Jesus Christ. So beyond the gift of teaching, we are called to teach.

> And the things that you have heard from me among many witnesses, commit these to faithful me who will be able to teach others also. (2 Timothy 2:2)

Bible Study Series

Most pastors use the scripture readings from the common lectionary as a guide when preparing their weekly sermons. A pastor also may be led to preach on topics like stewardship or family relationships or during seasons like Lent or Advent.

Generally, Bible studies are best taught in series. Since most churches do not have a set plan for choosing topics. Pastors are free to make choices that are best for the spiritual development of the ministry of the church. Some may use a book of the Bible, a biblical character, or a topic. God's plan was for his children to be taught in small increments:

> For precept must be up precept, precept upon precept, line upon line, line upon line; here a little and there a little. (Isaiah 28:10)

I have developed three categories of Bible studies in my ministries:

Books of the Bible
Christian Faith
The Bible in Today's World

Books of the Bible

Some books of the Bible are easier to read, understand, and study. Others, like Daniel, generate greater interest. It is recommended that all believers read the entire Bible from Genesis to Revelation. For some, this is an annual discipline; for others, they may complete this reading in three- to five-year cycles. It is not likely that you will hear of a study of the book of Numbers, but most certainly you'll hear of a study of the Gospel of St. John. Whichever book is chosen, the study of a Bible book builds knowledge and faith.

> Such things were written in the Scriptures long ago to teach us. And the scriptures give us hope and encouragement as we wait patiently for God's promises to be fulfilled. (Romans 15:4)

When studying the books of the Bible, one learns the following:

Context. The time, the audience, the culture, the history, and the reason for the writing.

Author: Who is he or she? Why was there a call of God from God? What is his or her background? What were the strengths and weaknesses?

Chapter and verse: What is the message? What are the important words and phrases? How does it relate to other messages in the Bible?

Relevance. How does this apply to my context, my church, my family, my life?

Christian Faith

Whether a new believer or a more mature believer, there is always something new to learn about faith in Jesus Christ. In a Christian context, where there is a diversity of beliefs and a wide range of Christian and emerging questionable doctrines, topical series can provide the biblical instruction for strengthening the faith. These topics can range from generally acceptable practices, like the Beatitudes, to interpretation of the Holy Spirit. There should necessarily be doctrinal matters that explain why we believe what we believe. The goal is not for everyone to agree but for everyone to search the scriptures for themselves.

For the time will come when people will no longer listen to sound and wholesome teaching. They will follow their own desires and will look for teachers who will tell them whatever their itching ears want to hear. (2 Timothy 4:3)

Teaching on the Christian faith helps in the following:

Instruction. Examine the Bible references. Engage views of writers or teachers on the topic.

Affirmation. Assure believers of their faith in God. Encourage them to grow.

Correction. Address false doctrines and beliefs. Expose the misinterpretations of scripture.

Practice. Challenge believers to practice what they have been taught.

❖ The Bible in Today's World

The church has often been criticized for its disconnect from the real issues of life. While pastors or leaders may not always be comfortable with every topic, remember that to avoid discussion is to allow members to get information from the wrong sources. We cannot afford to leave it to the schools, talk shows, books, and social media to teach us how to live in this ever-changing world.

> For if you remain silent at this time, relief and deliverance for the Jews will arise from another place, but you and your father's family will perish. And who knows but that you have come to your royal position for such a time as thing? (Esther 4:14 NIV)

We are to be the prophetic voice in the world. And while there are terms that may not be found in the scripture, topics on teaching the Bible in today's world help in:

Moral teaching—what does the Bible say about divorce, remarriage, gambling, etc.?

Legal/ethics—how do we engage legal matters, abortion, same-sex marriages, marijuana use?

Health—challenging the believers to financial, emotional, and physical health.

Bible Study Hour

In just one hour, there can be effective Bible study to meet the needs of the whole person—body, mind, and spirit. The following is the recommended structure of Bible study, but the importance of being sensitive to the Holy Spirit cannot be overemphasized.

Opening: Song/chorus, prayer, and welcome
Preview to New Series *or* Review of Last Lesson
Setting the Tone
Read the Text
Searching the Scriptures
Review
Closing: Song/offering/prayer/benediction

The opening exercise is to set the tone for worship. The presence of the Holy Spirit is acknowledged in the midst. In this way, the opening prayer is an invocation of the presence of the Holy Spirit and seeking God's direction for the study. A general welcome is good, as is a special acknowledgment of all visitors.

In the preview to the new series, the schedule is handed out with a stated objective. At this point, the rationale for the series should be noted. For example, it may be in response to a national crisis, like a natural disaster. Members' attention is drawn to any breaks due to holidays. Every class should begin with a review of the previous lessons. This is of benefit to those who were present as well as to those who were not in attendance.

One of the most useful yet challenging aspects of Bible study is to find an illustration that sets the tone for the study. I have included illustrations that may have been relevant at the time, but these can be changed for something that is more appropriate.

Reading the text for the day after setting the tone gives an enlightened perspective on the text. Now, you know where you are going and what to look for as you discuss the matters raised in setting the tone.

Then, the heart of the Bible study is the search of scriptures. The goal is to have as many relevant scriptures as possible to demonstrate the point. During this time, explanations are given. Other references may come up at the time. As members search the scriptures, the Spirit of God will bring further and deeper revelation of God's Word.

Every study should close with a review of the day's lesson. This will help members and those who may have been late to place the lesson in perspective.

The closing prayer could be intercessory, as members make requests. This is an appropriate time for an offering, if one is collected. The study closes with a benediction.

PART 2

Themes and Topics

CHAPTER 4

Books of The Bible

📖 **The Book of Ecclesiastes**

❖ **Introduction of a New Lesson**

Topic: How to Live Well—A Study of the Book of Ecclesiastes

Objective of Study: Many people work long and hard but never seem to enjoy the rewards of their labor. Many never seem to find any meaning in what they do. Many do not appreciate life and fail to live life to its fullness. This study of the book of Ecclesiastes is to give us the wisdom to live well. By the end of it, as believers, we should believe that it is God's will for us to live well, and we should follow his instructions in how to live well.

Duration: twelve lessons

❖ Schedule of Study

Lessons	Topic	Text
1	Is Life Worth Living?	Chapter 1
2	The Pleasures of Life	Chapter 2
3	Seasons of Life	Chapter 3
4	Relationship with Others	Chapter 4
5	Relationship with God	Chapter 5
6	Relationship with Things	Chapter 6
7	Reputation	Chapter 7
8	In Search of Wisdom	Chapter 8
9	Chance or Destiny?	Chapter 9
10	Don't Be a Fool	Chapter 10
11	Sowing and Reaping	Chapter 11
12	Honor God	Chapter 12

LESSON 1

📖 **Is Life Worth Living?**

❖ **Opening**

   ♣ **Background to the book**

   The book of Ecclesiastes was written by Solomon, the son of David. It was written later in Solomon's life. Solomon was looking back on a life of wealth, power, and influence. Although he asked God for wisdom, he did not always use it. His judgments were not always right. This book was written to those he loved and cared for so that they would not make the same mistakes as he did.

   ♣ **A key word throughout the book is *vanity*.** Vanity is the same word as for Abel. It means empty, meaningless, not lasting.

❖ **Set the Tone**

   ♣ **Thought:** A newspaper headline had the words, "The oldest man alive is ready to die." The story was about an old man in Indonesia who was proven to be 145 years. He had been saying that he just wanted to die. He had no desire to remain on this earth much longer.

   At 145, he had outlived all his siblings, four wives, all of his children.

   He had been preparing for his death for decades, and it still hadn't come.

   ♣ **Questions:** Why would he want to die? Do you think that he should be happy to go?

   There are sixty-five-, forty-five-, and twenty-five-year-olds who want to die. Should they feel this way?

   At different phases in life—but more especially the older you get—you think about life and wonder if it is worth it.

❖ Read the Text

Let us read the text: Ecclesiastes 1:1–18.

❖ Search the Scriptures

Life could be meaningless when we look at certain things.

♣ **Nothing is changing** (Ecclesiastes 1:3–7). Scientifically, there is no change.

References: The earth is God's creation (Genesis 1:1–2; 8:22; Psalm 24:1–2; Job 37:1–13; John 3:8).

♣ **Nothing is new in history** (Ecclesiastes 1:8–11). You can wear yourself out trying to find something new in history, but there is really nothing new.

References: Acts 17:16–30; Hebrews 13:8–9

♣ **Nothing is understood (philosophy)** (Ecclesiastes 1:12–18). The more you know, the more you realize you don't know. Our need is wisdom, which is the foundation for understanding and wisdom.

References: 1 Kings 4:29–34; Proverbs 9:10

❖ Closing

LESSON 2

📖 **The Pleasures of Life**

❖ **Opening**

❖ **Review of Previous Lesson**

❖ **Set the Tone**

   ♣ **Thought:** I met a member who was not bashful in saying publicly that she liked good things. She would testify that she came from humble beginnings and that God blessed her with enough wealth to enjoy her life. She built a nice home, bought quality clothing, and traveled all over the world. On her deathbed, she said to me that no one should cry for her because she knew Jesus Christ as Lord and Savior, and she had enjoyed life to the fullest.

   ♣ **Questions:** What does it mean to enjoy life to the fullest? Do you need earthly possessions? Is it acceptable to God to enjoy the pleasures of this world?

❖ **Read the Text**

Ecclesiastes 2:1–26

❖ **Search the Scriptures**

   ♣ **In search for happiness?** (Ecclesiastes: 2:1–11).

   References: Laughter (Job 8:20–21; Proverbs 14:13); Wine (Proverbs 31:4–7; Ephesians 5:18)

   Lifestyle of the famous (2 Chronicles 8:1–6; Luke 12:15–21).

   ♣ **Hating life:** Ecclesiastes 2:12–23

   References: All will die (Psalm 49:5–13); troubled by life (1 Kings 19:3–4); had to leave everything (1 Timothy 6:6–8)

   ♣ **Enjoy the now** (Ecclesiastes 2:24–26).

   Enjoy what you have (Philippians 4:11–13). Trust God (1 Timothy 6:17–19).

❖ **Closing**

📖 **Seasons of Life**

❖ **Review of Lessons**

❖ **Set the Tone**

Thought: A recent high school graduate was asked why he was no longer attending the youth activities of the church. He responded, "I am too old for that. That was so 'last year.'"

Questions: What in our lives feels like it was so "last year"? Do we feel like we have passed certain seasons in life?

❖ **Read the Text**

Ecclesiastes 3:1–22

❖ **Search the Scripture**

♣ **Time for everything** (Ecclesiastes 3:1–8).

♦ **References:** Fourteen seasons

Birth and death: Job 1:21
Plant and reap: Galatians 6:7–9
Kill and heal: 1 Samuel 2:6
Tear down and build up; cry and laugh: Psalm 30:5
Grieve and dance: Jeremiah 31:13
Scatter stones and gather stones: 2 Kings 3:25
Embrace and turn away: Luke 15:20
Search and quit searching: Jeremiah 45:5
Keep and throw away: Ephesians 4:20–24
Tear down and mend: Jeremiah 1:10
Quiet and speak: James 1:19
Love and hate: Psalm 97:10
War and peace: Isaiah 2:4

♣ **God's time:** Ecclesiastes 3:9–15

References: God's time (Romans 8:28); don't worry; be happy (Matthew 6:25–34); fear God (Proverbs 14:26)

♣ **Injustices in life**: Ecclesiastes 3:16–22

References: Psalm 146:3–9; Isaiah 56:1

📖 **Relationship with Others**

❖ **Review**

❖ **Set the Tone**

    ♣ **Thoughts:** On the radio program *Focus on the Family*, the guest speaker said that the key to fulfilment in life is having healthy relationships with others. Whether you have a good job, talents, or wealth, you would have failed at life if you failed at relationships.

    ♣ **Questions:** What do you think about this? Do you believe that you have good relationships?

❖ **Read the Text**

Ecclesiastes 4:1–16
Search the Scriptures

    ♣ **Neighbors**—Ecclesiastes 4:4–6

    References: Do not covet (Exodus 20:17; Acts 20:33–35); love (Matthew 19:16–19; Proverbs 3:29–30; Romans 13:9–10)

    ♣ **Companions** (Ecclesiastes 4:7–12)

    References: Fruitful (Genesis 1:27–28; Psalm 127); helper (Genesis 2:18; Proverbs 18:22)

    ♣ **Advisors:** Ecclesiastes 4:13–16

    References: Accepting counsel (Proverbs 19:20; Exodus 18:13–21); refusing to listen (Acts 27:18–22; 2 Chronicles 25:15–16)

LESSON 5

📖 **Relationship with God**

❖ **Review of Lesson**

❖ **Set the Tone**

  ♣ **Thought:** Generally, a relationship with God can be in three ways: (1) We have no relationship with God. We either do not acknowledge that there is a God (atheist), or we believe that there is no way of knowing that there is a God (agnostic); (2) We have a casual relationship with God. We know that there is a God. We may worship him on some occasions, but we are not dependent on God; (3) We have a personal relationship with God. We acknowledge God to be Sovereign, and we live our lives depending fully on God.

  ♣ **Questions:** What kind of relationship is pleasing to the Lord? How do we nurture our relationship with God?

Read the Text
Ecclesiastes 5:1–19

❖ **Search the Scriptures**

  ♣ Approach to God (Ecclesiastes 5:1–7).

    References: In silence (Habakkuk 2:20; Zephaniah 1:7; Psalm 46:10); honor promises and prayers (Proverbs 20:25; Matthew 5:33–36; James 5:15); empty words (Matthew 6:7; Psalm 5:1–6)

  ♣ God through the eyes of society (Ecclesiastes 5:8–15).

    References: Oppression of the poor (Deuteronomy 24:17–18); love of money (Hebrews 13:5; 1 Timothy 6:9–10).

  ♣ Life is short (Ecclesiastes 5:16–20).

    References: Wealth (Deuteronomy 8:18; Proverbs 8:17–21); health (3 John 1:2; Proverbs 10:22).

❖ **Closing**

📖 **Relationship with Things**

❖ **Opening**

❖ **Review of Lesson**

❖ **Set the Tone**

♣ **Thought**: In a village, a hardworking man spent most of his life trying to build his dream home. He finished building the home just before he retired. About a week after he moved into his new home, he died. Since his only child was living in another country, the house was left unoccupied for a long time. As villagers passed there daily, they would be saddened by the thought that he did not even get the chance to enjoy the fruit of his labor.

♣ **Questions:** What do think about this situation? Was this a punishment from God? Is this life?

❖ **Read the Text**

Ecclesiastes 6:1–12

❖ **Search the Scriptures**

♣ Wealth and enjoyment (Ecclesiastes 6:1–2)

   References: Job 31:24–28; Proverbs 30:7–9; Proverbs 11:4, 28
   How will life end? (Ecclesiastes 6:3–6).
   References: Psalm 49:16–19; Isaiah 14:18–20; Job 3:11–26
   Eternal investment (Ecclesiastes 6:10–12).
   References: Luke 9:23–25; 12:29–34; Revelation 3:17–21

❖ **Closing**

📖 **Reputation**

❖ **Opening**

❖ **Review of Lessons**

❖ **Set the Tone**

Thought: When the abuse scandal of actor Bill Cosby became known, many of us were saddened. For two decades, he was the model family man on television—the loving husband and father. He was an inspiration to those of African descent who believed that they could be lawyers, doctors, and homeowners. Unfortunately, it was difficult to celebrate that after learning of the horrible stories associated with him.

Questions: Has he lost his reputation for you? Do scandals affect reputation? Does a discovery of immoral behavior affect good work?

❖ **Read the Text**

Ecclesiastes 7:1–27

❖ **Search the Scriptures**

♣ **Maintain integrity** (Ecclesiastes 7:1–9).

References: 2 Samuel 22:26–27; Job 2:3; Acts 5:1–11; Psalm 25:19–21

♣ **Living now** (Ecclesiastes 7:10–18).

References: James 1:4–8; Philippians 2:2–8; Psalm 23

♣ **Be virtuous** (Ecclesiastes 7:19–29).

References: 2 Peter 1:1–1; Proverbs 31:10–31

❖ **Closing**

LESSON 8

📖 **In Search of Wisdom**

❖ **Opening**

❖ **Review of Lessons**

❖ **Set the Tone**

♣ **Thought:** With the advancement of aviation engineering, flights are heavily dependent on a computerized system. We may not be able to get our heads around the idea that flights can be flown in autopilot. The system has all the necessary components and can guide the flight safely toward its destination. These are the smart or the wise systems.

♣ **Questions:** What do we depend on to help us navigate through the clouds of life? What instruments do we use to help us to make the right decisions? Do we depend on the wisdom of God?

❖ **Read the Text**

Ecclesiastes 8:1–17
Our human wisdom is limited, and that is why we need God's wisdom to make sense of life.

❖ **Search the Scriptures**

♣ **Civil duty** (Ecclesiastes 8:1–8).

References: 1 Chronicles 29:23–24; Romans 13:1–7; Matthew 22:15–22

♣ **Justice will be served** (Ecclesiastes 8:9–15).

References: Amos 5:23–24; Micah 6: 8; Psalm 37:27–29; Proverbs 21:15

♣ **The godly will be rewarded** (Ecclesiastes 8:14–17).

References: Psalm 73:1–20; Proverbs 23:17–18; Psalm 1

❖ **Closing**

LESSON 9

📖 **Chance or Destiny?**

❖ **Opening**

❖ **Review of Lessons**

❖ **Set the Tone**

♣ **Thought:** When we were leaving Tanzania, we saw a group of African children and parents who were immigrating to the United States. We were told that they were part of the International Organization for Migration. Not only did they get special treatment in the US, but when we landed in Qatar, they were also well taken care of. This was very good for them.

♣ **Questions:** When one thinks of the millions of Africans living in poverty, war, and suffering, how did they choose these few? Why do some people get a break and not others? Do you believe in chance or coincidence?

❖ **Read the Text**

Ecclesiastes 9:1–17
The wise man continues to work through issues, understanding which issues we have control over and which we don't.

❖ **Search the Scriptures**

♣ **Favor of God (**Ecclesiastes 9:1–4).

References: Psalm 84:11; Proverbs 12:2–3; Matthew 5:45

♣ **Live before you die** (Ecclesiastes 9:5–12; Hebrews 9:27; Philippians 1:20–24; Proverbs 18:22; 5:18–20).

♣ **Wisdom is precious** (Proverbs 3:13–15; 14:33–34).

❖ **Closing**

LESSON 10

📖 **Don't Be a Fool**

❖ **Opening**

❖ **Review of Lessons**

❖ **Set the Tone**

Thought: You can fool all the people some of the time and some of the people all the time, but you cannot fool all the people all the time.—Abraham Lincoln

Questions: What does it mean to fool someone? How do you describe a fool?

❖ **Read the Lesson**

  ♣ **The Foolish** (Ecclesiastes 10:1–4).

    References: Proverbs 18:2; 4:23

  ♣ **Foolish rulers** (Ecclesiastes 10:5–7).

    References: 1 Kings 3:3–28; Proverbs 30:21–23

  ♣ **Foolish workers** (Ecclesiastes 10:8–15).

    References: Matthew 25:1–13; Colossians 3:23

  ♣ **Foolish officers** (Ecclesiastes 10:16–20).

    References: Isaiah 3:1–5; 1 Timothy 3:6

❖ **Closing**

LESSON 11

📖 **Sowing and Reaping**

❖ **Opening**

❖ **Review of Previous Lessons**

❖ **Set the Tone**

♣ **Thought:** The economic recession of 2008 was devastating for many. Some persons lost their homes and investments. There were promises of helping people to keep their homes and some of their investments, but this did not always work out.

♣ **Questions:** What are the lessons to be learned from economic recession? How are people able to recover from financial losses?

❖ **Read the Scripture**

Ecclesiastes 11:1–10

❖ **Search the Scriptures**

Generous giving (Ecclesiastes 11:1–3)
References: Leviticus 19:23–25; Deuteronomy 15:7–11; Proverbs 19:17; Luke 6:38
Sow by faith (Ecclesiastes 11:4–6).
References: Genesis 26:1–14; Psalm 126:6; Galatians 6:7–9; 2 Corinthians 9:6–11
Enjoy your youth (Ecclesiastes 11:7–10).
References: Isaiah 46:3–4; Ruth 4:15; Psalm 37:25–26

❖ **Closing**

📖 **Honor God**

❖ **Opening**

❖ **Review of Lessons**

❖ **Set the Tone**:

♣ **Thought:** There is a wide variety of behavior among the elderly, especially in nursing homes. Some elderly always seem to have joy. They have smiles on their faces and sing hymns and songs. Others are quiet, with nothing much to say. Yet others appear irritable or stubborn and resist the care given to them.

♣ **Questions:** Do you think that those who work with the elderly can tell anything about their early lives, based on their present behavior? Do you think a godly life in youth can be seen in the lives of the elderly?

❖ **Read the Text**

Ecclesiastes 12:1–14

❖ **Search the Scriptures**

♣ **Remember God in youth** (Ecclesiastes 12:1–7).

References: Psalm 119: 9–11; Proverbs 22:6; 1 Tim 4:12–13

♣ **Knowing the truth** (Ecclesiastes 12:8–12).

References: Psalm 25:4–5; John 8:31–32; 14:6; 2 Timothy 2:15

♣ **Fear and obey God** (Ecclesiastes 12:8–14).

References: Deuteronomy 6:24; Psalm 128:1–4; Luke 1:50

Closing

THE BOOK OF HOSEA

📖 **Introduction of a New Lesson**

Topic: The Faithfulness of God—A Study of the Book of Hosea

Objective: In life, we all make commitments—to relationships, to organizations, to worthy causes, to ourselves, and to God. At some point, all of us fail to fulfill our commitments. At times, our failures can be easily corrected with an apology, but there are times when our broken commitments result in difficult-to-repair strains. The book of Hosea shows us that despite our failures, unfaithfulness, and sins, God is faithful to us. The purpose of this study is to give us hope, even when we have failed God.

Duration: twelve lessons

❖ **Schedule of Study**

Lessons	Topic	Text
1	Hosea: A Family Man	Hosea 1:1–11
2	Unfaithful Partner	Hosea 2:1–13
3	Unfaithful People	Hosea 2:14–13
4	Loving the Unfaithful	Hosea 3:1–5
5	Addicted to Sin	Hosea 4:1–19
6	The Sins of Leaders	Hosea 5: 1–15
7	The Healing of God	Hosea 6:1–7:16
8	Forgetting God	Hosea 8:1–14
9	Consequences of Sin	Hosea 9–10
10	God's Unfailing Love	Hosea 11:1–11
11	Giving an Account to God	Hosea 12–13
12	Forgiveness Lifts Burdens	Hosea 14:1–9

LESSON 1

📖 **Hosea: A Family Man**

❖ **Opening**

❖ **Review of Lesson**

❖ **Set the Tone**

♣ **Thought:** The neighbors in a village observed a very devoted Christian man who loved his wife and their three children. He worked at a hotel, and after a long day at work, he would come home and work hard at home. His wife, who was not employed outside of the home at the time, was known to be unfaithful to her loving husband. One day, when he was coming home from work, he saw her on her way to meet with her outside friend. He asked her to come back home, but she insisted on going. That evening, she got into a very bad accident and was in a coma. Her husband was at her bedside, holding his wife and crying out, "Lord, don't take my wife." She recovered after several months of hospitalization and rehabilitation. But after a while, she went back to her old ways.

♣ **Questions:** If you were this husband, what would you have done? Do you think it's unfair for such a kind man to find himself in such a situation?

❖ **Read the Text**

Hosea 1:1–11

❖ **Search the Scriptures**

♣ **Hosea's background** (Hosea 1:1). He was a prophet who served during the reign of Jeroboam II, the king of Israel. At this time, Israel was doing well economically, but the people had become worldly. They had given up God for the things of the world. The Lord raised up Hosea to minister to them.

Hosea's name means salvation. His father's name was Beeri. Many scholars believe that Hosea was a farmer because he spoke a lot about beasts, fig trees, and life in the country.

References: 2 Kings 14:23–27; Hosea 10:12

♣ **Marriage** (Hosea 1:2–3). God told Hosea to marry a prostitute. Hosea wife's name was Gomer, the daughter of Diblaim. This was a symbolic marriage to demonstrate the unfaithfulness of God's children.

References: Deuteronomy 23:17–18; Hosea 9:10

Children (Hosea 1:3–9). There are three children.

Name and Meaning
Jezreel Scattered Avenge bloodshed at Jezreel 2 Kings 10:11
Lo-ruhamah Not loved Mercy for Judah and not Israel. Isaiah 30:18
Lo-ammi Not my people God disowning His people. Isaiah 63:16

Perhaps all three children were not Hosea's biological children. However, God has promised restoration.

Restoration (Hosea 1:10–11).

Reference: Joel 2:25–27; Acts 3:19–21

❖ **Closing**

📖 **Unfaithful Partner**

❖ **Opening**

❖ **Review of Last Lesson**

❖ **Set the Tone**

Thought: Story of Unfaithfulness

It is very hard to tell people what to do in the case of unfaithfulness. The deepest pain, hurt, disappointment, and broken hearts in relationships are usually a result of unfaithfulness. Most people are married because they expect their partners to be faithful to them. But hard as it appears, unfaithfulness is not the unforgiveable sin.

Questions: How can a couple deal with unfaithfulness? Could life be the same after unfaithfulness?

❖ **Read the Text**

Hosea 2:1–13

❖ **Search the Scriptures**

♣ **Ultimatum:** Enough is enough (Hosea 2:1–5).

Hosea disowns her. He asks her to take off her makeup, seductive clothing, and jewelry. Otherwise, he will not take care of her children.

References: Ezekiel 23:1–21; 1 Corinthians 5:1–5

♣ **Intervention:** Hosea 2:6–8

Hosea sets boundaries for his wife.

References: Numbers 22:21–33; 1 Corinthians 6:12–13

♣ **Consequences to actions** (Hosea 2:9–13).

The privileges that Gomer had were taken away.

References: Ezekiel 23:28–35; Hebrews 12:6

❖ **Closing**

📖 **Unfaithful People**

❖ **Opening**

❖ **Review of Last Lesson**

❖ **Set the Tone**

Thought: In the early years of Moravian missions, a young missionary and his wife felt called to start missions in a remote area in Tanzania. They spent much time among the people and served them with great sacrifice. The people began to understand what it is to be Christian. They gave up their religious practices. The missionaries taught them to read and write. They put local leaders in charge.

But when the two missionaries took ill, they had to leave, and there was no immediate replacement for them. When they returned a year later, what do you think they found? Most of the people had gone back to their old ways and wanted to hear nothing about the gospel. The missionaries felt discouraged and wanted to give up, but God gave them the strength. One by one, people came back, the mission expanded, and today, it is one of the most populated missions.

Questions: What are the things that lead us away from God? How challenging is it to hold on to your faith?

❖ **Read the Text**

> Hosea 2:14–24

❖ **Search the Scriptures**

♣ **Wilderness experience** (Hosea 2:14–15). The desert is the wilderness experience. We know that the children of Israel were in the wilderness, and it was a place where the Lord could speak with them.

References: Genesis 21:14–18; Jeremiah 2:1–3

♣ **Renewed covenant** (Hosea 2:16–20).

What is the difference between husband "ishi" and Master "Ba-ali"? The difference is faithfulness, loyalty.

References: Jeremiah 31:31–34; Ezekiel 36:26–27

♣ **Times of refreshing** (Hosea 2:21–23).

Only God can refresh the dryness and weariness of life. God will bring blessings even upon those who did not belong to him, the Gentiles (Isaiah 44:1–5; John 4:13–14).

❖ **Closing**

📖 **Loving the Unfaithful**

❖ **Opening**

❖ **Review**

❖ **Set the Tone**

Thought: Adults and children alike have had the experience of forgetting their lunch containers at work or at school. Usually, as a precaution, you will go the extra mile to disinfect the containers, probably soaking them overnight.

Questions: How do you treat things that have gone missing? How do you treat loved ones who may have developed unpleasant habits?

❖ **Read the Text**

Hosea 3:1–5

❖ **Search the Scriptures**

♣ **Undeserved love of God** (Hosea 3:1). God reaches out to us because of his love for us.

References: Lamentations 3:22–23; Jeremiah 31:3; Psalm 86:15–17; Romans 5:6–9

♣ **Redemption** (Hosea 3:2–3). God purchases us back from the ownership of our enemies.

References: John 15:13–17; 1 Peter 1:17–20; 1 Corinthians 6:18–20

♣ **Repentance** (Hosea 3:4–5). God requires that we change our ways.

References: 2 Chronicles 7:13–14; Proverbs 28:13; Matthew 9:12–13; 1 John 1:8–10

❖ **Closing**

LESSON 5

📖 **Addicted to Sin**

❖ **Opening**

❖ **Review of Last Lesson**

❖ **Set the Tone**

Thought: After two marriages and divorces, a pastor decided that he would get professional help before he married a third time. As a result of the counseling session, he realized his flaws, bad habits, mistakes, and sins. He better understood why he did what he did.

Questions: How well do we know ourselves? Do we understand what drives us to unhealthy and immoral behavior?

❖ **Read the Text**

Hosea 4:1–19

❖ **Search the Scripture**

♣ **Ungodliness** (Hosea 4:1–3). There is widespread unrighteousness and immoral behavior across the land.

References: Proverbs 14:34; Isaiah 65:11–12; Ephesians 5:1–5

♣ **Failure of priests as bad examples** (Hosea 4:4–10). The sins of the spiritual leaders corrupt the whole body.

References: Jeremiah 23:9–12; Ezekiel 34:2–10, Isaiah 5:11–12, 1 Peter 5:2–4

♣ **Fatal combination of alcoholism and prostitution** (Hosea 4:11–19).

References: Proverbs 20:1; 31:4–5; 6:24–27; Romans 13:11–14

Closing

LESSON 6

📖 **The Sins of the Leaders**

❖ **Opening**

❖ **Review of Lessons**

❖ **Set the Tone**

Thought: From Roman Catholic priests to evangelical pastors, there is no secret that pastors have fallen from grace. Many wonder if they were insincere from the beginning or if they had a moment of weakness.

Questions: Are priests/pastors who fail wicked or weak? How do you trust pastors when they have failed?

❖ **Read the Text**

    Hosea 5:1–15

❖ **Search the Scriptures**

    ♣ **Spirit of idolatry** (Hosea 5:1–4). God is a jealous God and would have no other worship but worship of him.

        References: Exodus 20:2–6; Psalm 16:2–4; Romans 1:24–25

    ♣ **Spirit of arrogance** (Hosea 5:5–9). There are too many leaders who are full of themselves.

        References: 2 Kings 5:1–15; Mark 10:42–45; Romans 12:3

    ♣ **Spirit of corruption** (Hosea 5:10–15). Corruption is losing the sense of right or wrong (Isaiah 5:20–23; Luke 19:6–8; Ephesians 4:28).

❖ **Closing**

LESSON 7

📖 **The Healing of God**

❖ **Opening**

❖ **Review**

❖ **Set the Tone**

Thought: A commercial that comes on the local TV station every evening says that if you have problems in your marriage, are sick, or need a relationship restored, call this number for prayer. The source of the commercial is not clear—whether it's an established church, a ministry, or even a non-Christian organization.

Questions: What would be your response to the commercial? Is this a number you would call if you needed healing?

❖ **Read the Text**

Hosea 6:1–7:16

❖ **Search the Scriptures**

♣ **Broken pieces restored:** Healing is putting broken pieces back together.

References: Jeremiah 18:1–5; Psalm 147:1–3; 51:17

♣ **Getting back to God:** Many want to be healed by God, but they don't want God (Hosea 6:7–11).

References: Jeremiah 17:14; James 5:13–16; Luke 17:11–17

♣ **God sees the heart** (Hosea 7:1–10). There must be sincerity in our hearts to receive the healing of God and live as we like.

References: Exodus 15:24–26; Psalm 103:1–5; Psalm 51:7–10

♣ **Breaking the chain of rebellion.** When we get comfortable with a sinful, rebellious life, it is hard to break that chain.

References: 1 Samuel 15:23; Hebrews 3:12–15; James 1:22–25

❖ **Closing**

LESSON 8

 📖 **Forgetting God**

❖ **Opening**

❖ **Review**

❖ **Set the Tone**

Thought: One of the medical mysteries is the early onset of Alzheimer's disease. There was a feature on CBS television on the increase of persons in their early fifties who have full-blown Alzheimer's. Now, it is linked to a gene. Once upon a time, this was disease for people in their eighties and nineties. Families have said that it is one of the most painful things when someone you love doesn't know who you are.

Questions: Have you experienced Alzheimer's with a loved one? What was your experience? How does it feel to know that, as a spouse or a child, your loved one has forgotten you?

God accused Israel of forgetting God and choosing to replace God with other things.

❖ **Read the Text**

Read Hosea 8:1–14

❖ **Search the Scriptures**

  ♣ **Forgot the law** (Hosea 8:1–4)

    The Lord established a law so that the people of God could live godly lives, but they forgot the law.

    References: Exodus 20:1–17; Proverbs 3:1–4; Matthew 5:17–19

♣ **Forgot about true worship** (Hosea 8:5–10)

Instead of worshipping God, they worshipped idols. God wants us to worship him alone

References: Exodus 23:24–25; Habakkuk 3:17–18; John 4:21–24

♣ **Forgot their Maker**

God reminds us that he is our Maker (Psalm 100:1–3; 95:6–7; Nehemiah 9:6).

❖ **Closing**

LESSON 9

📖 **Consequences of Sin**

❖ **Opening**

❖ **Review of Lesson**

❖ **Set the Tone**

Thought: It is said that if you have a good lawyer, you can get away with anything. A good lawyer can use the law to keep you from paying the price of your actions. You may not be innocent, but a good lawyer finds a way for you to avoid punishment. But when it comes to the Lord, it is not the same.

Questions: Do you think that lawyers know if their clients are guilty? Would you go to a lawyer to help you avoid punishment for your actions?

❖ **Read the Text**

Hosea 9:1–10:10
When we continue to live in a way that is displeasing to God, we suffer the consequences.

❖ **Search the Scriptures**

♣ **Scarcity** (Hosea 9:1–4). They would not have enough food to eat or to present unto the Lord.

References: Lamentations 4:9, Haggai 1:3–6, Acts 7:9–11

♣ **Loss** (Hosea 9:5–14). When God is not our side, we stand to lose our battles.

Leviticus 26:14–17; Isaiah 47:8–11; Acts 27:21–26

♣ **Judgment** (Hosea 9:15–10:10). God will be the final judge (Isaiah 26: 7–9; Matthew 12:26; 33–37; Revelation 20:11–15).

❖ **Closing**

LESSON 10

📖 **God's Unfailing Love**

❖ **Opening**

❖ **Review**

❖ **Set the Tone**

Thought: Cultures approach parenting differently. In Western cultures, children are expected to be independent by their early twenties. Parents plan for their own futures, including senior care, and hardly expect their children to assist. In non-Western cultures, parents have no problem with limitless assistance for their children. At the same time, if children become independent, they are expected to take care of their parents who made sacrifices for them.

Questions: Which parenting style is better? Which one better reflects God's parenting style?

❖ **Read the Text**

> Hosea 10:11–11:11
> This chapter focuses on God's parental love. God continues to love us as a parent.

❖ **Search the Scriptures**

♣ **Children make their own choices** (Hosea 10:11–15). Even when righteous seeds are planted, children choose to do what they want.

References: 1 Samuel 2:12–17, 22–25; Luke 15:11–19

♣ **God's love is unconditional** (Hosea 11:1–4). It was God who taught us everything. He holds us in his heart.

References: Isaiah 49:15–16; 41:11–13; Luke 13:34

♣ **God will rescue his own** (Hosea 11: 5–11; Exodus 3:7–10; Daniel 6:16–23; Psalm 34:17).

❖ **Closing**

LESSON 11

📖 **Love and Justice**

❖ **Opening**

❖ **Review of Lessons**

❖ **Set the Tone**

Thought: In a court of law, families and loved ones hope for justice. Justice might mean that the accused is penalized for the alleged crime, but justice also might mean that the accused is set free.

Questions: What does it mean when we say justice is served? Is it possible for a human judge to serve justice?

❖ **Read the Text**

Read Hosea 11:12–13:3
God lives by the principles of love and justice.

❖ **Search the Scriptures**

♣ **The Story of Jacob** (Hosea 11:12–12:6)

References: Genesis 25:21–26 (struggle in the womb); Genesis 27:1–27 (deception); Genesis 28:13–17 (at Bethel)

♣ **The deception of prosperity** (Hosea 12:7–14). It is not right to assume that your financial wealth is an approval from God.

References: Deuteronomy 8:11–20; Luke 12:16–21; James 3:13–16

♣ **Losing your moral authority** (Hosea 13:1–3). When you have sinned, it is difficult for others to look up to you. (Judges 16:1–31).

❖ **Closing**

LESSON 12

📖 **Forgiveness**

❖ **Opening**

❖ **Review of Lessons**

❖ **Set the Tone**

Thought: A widow wrote her will and left most of her worldly goods to her niece. The widow did not have children of her own, but she and her late husband had raised the niece.

The widow later became disappointed with the niece. She had relocated to another country and did not call or visit. The widow decided to change her will and to divide her possessions among others. When the niece learned of this change of plan, she apologized to her aunt for her wayward behavior and asked for her forgiveness.

Questions: Should the widow change her will again? Does forgiveness restore all the promised blessings?

❖ **Read the Text**

> Hosea 13:4–14:9
> The last chapter of Hosea talks about the promises God has for his people if we return to him.

❖ **Search the Scriptures**

♣ **God's forgiveness** (Hosea 13:4–4:2)

What's the difference between God's forgiveness and ours? As long as we come to God, he will forgive (Isaiah 1:18–20; Psalm 103:1–13; Matthew 6:14).

♣ **God's favor** (Hosea 14:3–7).

When we experience God's forgiveness, we walk in his favor. *Favor* is to have God's undeserved blessings and success in our lives (Genesis 39:2–4; Numbers 6:22–26; Ephesians 1:3–8).

♣ **God's fruitfulness**

The fruit of God is fruit that will last (Psalm 1, John 15:1–17, Galatians 5:22–23).

❖ **Closing**

❖ **Introduction of New Lesson**

❖ **The Secret of Lasting Joy**

❖ **Objective**

To show the believer that the joy of the Lord is not dependent upon outward circumstances. Whether we are in a season of plenty or a season of need, our joy in Christ will not waver. It is that joy that gives us strength for life's journey.

❖ **Duration of Study: ten lessons**

❖ **Schedule**

Lessons	Topic	Scripture Reading
1	What Is the Secret?	Philippians 1:1–6
2	Joy in Serving	Philippians 1:7–19
3	Joy in Suffering	Philippians 1:20–30
4	Joyful Attitude	Philippians 2:1–11
5	Rejoicing with Others	Philippians 2:12–18
6	Joy in Following	Philippians 2:19–30
7	Be Careful to Keep Joy	Philippians 3:1–11
8	Joy in Faithfulness	Philippians 3:12–21
9	Joy in Working with Others	Philippians 4:1–9
10	Joy in Giving	Philippians 4:10–23

LESSON 1

📖 **What Is the Secret?**

❖ **Opening**

❖ **Introduction to New Lesson**

❖ **Set the Tone**

    ♣ **Thought:** I received an email with the subject "Sad news." It was from a wonderful couple we'd met in the United States, whose father/father-in-law had passed during the night. He was eighty-nine. They were sad to report that he had passed on but were happy to know that he had passed in his own home, in his own bed, with his family by his side.

    ♣ **Questions:** Was this sad news or good news? What makes you sad? What makes you happy?

❖ **Read the Text**

Philippians 1:1–6

    ♣ **Background to the Study:** The apostle Paul wrote a letter around AD 61 to the Christians at Philippi. This church was started by Paul and his missionary companions while they were on their second missionary journey. Philippi was the first European church. While in prison, this church sent Paul a gift, which he appreciated. He then sent a letter of thanksgiving and to encourage them to hold on in their faith in God by having the true joy of the Lord.

❖ **Search the Scriptures**

    ♣ **Personal letter** (Philippians 1:1–2). Paul wrote a personal letter on Timothy's and his behalf. He wrote to the believers and the leaders in the church.

    References: Acts 16:11–40; 1 Timothy 3:1–13

♣ **Praying for fellow believers** (Philippians 1:3–4). He thanked God for them and prayed always for them (Job 42:10; Romans 1:8–9; Ephesians 6:18–20).

♣ **Faithful Christian partners** (Philippians 1:5–6). They were working with him. Some of the other churches were working against him. It is good to know when people are working with you (1 Corinthians 1:9; Galatians 6:9).

❖ **Closing**

📖 Joy in Serving

❖ Opening

❖ Review of Lesson

❖ Set the Tone

♣ **Thought:** There are many newly formed ministries. While some reach new converts, most attract members of other denominations. The preachers are usually passionate about their missions and believe that God has called them to proclaim his Word in a way that others may not be able to do.

♣ **Questions:** What do you think of the rise of new preachers today? Do you think that God is glorified with all that they are doing?

❖ Read the Text

Philippians 1:7–19

♣ **Background to lesson**

Paul wanted the believers to keep their attention on the Christian principles by which they had lived. They needed to focus on what mattered.

❖ Search the Scriptures

♣ **Defending the truth** (Jude 1:3; 1 Peter 3:15).

♣ **Knowledge and understanding** (Proverbs 4:7, 2 Peter 3:18).

♣ **Bear fruit** (John 15:16; Galatians 5:22–23).

♣ **Preach Christ** (Philippians 12–19). Despite some questionable motives, the important thing is that the gospel is being preached. Mandate (Mark 16:15; Acts 1:8). Need (Jonah 1:1–2; Ephesians 3:7–9). It's good news (Isaiah 55:10–11; Romans 10:14–17; 1 Corinthians 17–18).

❖ Closing

LESSON 3

📖 **Joy in Suffering**

❖ **Opening**

❖ **Review**

❖ **Set the Tone**

♣ **Thought:** Christian author and psychologist James Dobson tells the story of a time when his mother was undergoing tests to see if she had cancer. He eventually got the results from the doctor and took them to his mother, saying, "Mom, I have good news. The doctor said that there is no cancer." A few days later, his mother said to him, "I was not happy about the news because I was looking forward to seeing your dad again and being with the Lord."

♣ **Questions:** What do you think of this story? What makes news good or bad?

❖ **Read the Text**

Philippians 1:20–30
These verses from Paul represent the kind of struggle he had as he came to grips with his own death.

❖ **Search the Scriptures**

♣ **Two desires** (Philippians 1:20–25) Death or life—which one is better?

References: 2 Kings 20:1–21; Psalm 116:15; Galatians 2:19–20; 2 Corinthians 5:6–9; Revelation 14:13

♣ **Suffering together** (Philippians 1:27–30)

In preaching the gospel, there will be suffering. But the saints of God are encouraged to join together in their sufferings (Isaiah 53:1–3; John 16:31–33; 1 Peter 4:12–19; Romans 5:1–5).

❖ **Closing**

LESSON 4

📖 **Joyful Attitude**

❖ **Opening**

❖ **Review of Lessons**

❖ **Set the Tone**

    ♣ **Thought:** It is no secret that one's attitude determines one's altitude. This is true for the student, the athlete, the unemployed, and the sick person.

    ♣ **Questions:** What is considered a good or bad attitude? How do we get our attitude?

❖ **Read the Text**

Philippians 2:1–11
In this text, Paul shows them that they need the attitude of Christ.

❖ **Search the Scripture**

    ♣ **Right attitude** (Philippians 2:1–2).

    Encouragement, comfort, fellowship, and compassion bring agreement, love, and unity.

    References: John 17:22–26; 1 Peter 3:8–9; 1 Corinthians 1:10–17; Galatians 3:26–29

    ♣ **Wrong attitude** (Philippians 2:3–4). Let us not be arrogant or selfish.

    References: Mark 10:35–45; Luke 14:7–11; Romans 12: 3

    ♣ **Attitude of Christ** (Philippians 2:5–11).

    References: Isaiah 53:7–12; John 1:1–5; 2 Corinthians 8:9

❖ **Closing**

LESSON 5

📖 **Rejoicing with Others**

❖ **Opening**

❖ **Review of Lessons**

❖ **Set the Tone**

    ♣ **Thought:** A good coach is an important part of a team. A coach trains and prepares the team for competition. But on game day, the team has to play for itself. If the players do well and have applied all the instructions in practice, then the coach is pleased. When the team forgets the instructions, the coach is upset. Teachers, preachers, leaders, and pastors have served as coaches in the lives of many teams.

    ♣ **Questions:** What should be our response when our team plays well? Do we blame ourselves when our team fails?

❖ **Read the Text**

Philippians 2:12–18
Paul says to the church that he has coached them, and they should give him every reason to rejoice.

❖ **Search the Scripture**

    ♣ **Work hard** (Philippians 2:12–13). We have to work hard at our relationship with God.

    References: Psalm 128:1–2; Ecclesiastes 3:22; John 6:26–27; Colossians 3:23–26

    ♣ **Work willingly** (Philippians 2:14–15). The Christian should press on without murmuring or complaining.

    References: Numbers 14:26–30; 1 Corinthians 10:10; James 5:9

♣ **Work tirelessly** (Philippians 2:16–18). Continue to do good, even when you are physically tired.

References: Isaiah 40:28–31; Matthew 11:28–30; Galatians 6:9; 2 Timothy 4:6–7

❖ **Closing**

LESSON 6

📖 **Joy in Following**

❖ **Opening**

❖ **Review of Lessons**

❖ **Set the Tone**

   ♣ **Thought:** If you are a leader, you should also be a follower.

   ♣ **Questions:** What do you think of the above statement? Can you lead and also follow?

❖ **Read the Text**

Philippians 2:19–30
Paul's greatest joy was in knowing that some of the disciples could continue the work in his absence.

❖ **Search the Scripture**

   ♣ **Timothy** (Philippians 2:19–24). Paul chose Timothy because of the Christlike qualities he brought to ministry.

   References: Acts 15:36–16:5; 2 Timothy 1:3–7; 1 Corinthians 4:14–17

   ♣ **Epaphroditus** (Philippians 2:25–30). He was the armor-bearer for Paul. He was the one who delivered the original manuscript of the letter to the believers while Paul was imprisoned. He did much more than what he was asked to do. He got sick and almost died. Paul appreciated his ministry. He was called a true brother, true fellow worker, and a true soldier.

   References: Philippians 4:18; Exodus 17:10–12; Mark 14:30–31; 1 Corinthians 3:7–9

❖ **Closing**

📖 **Preserving Your Joy**

❖ **Opening**

❖ **Review**

❖ **Set the Tone**

♣ **Thought:** John, a young Christian professional, gave God thanks for the way God was working in his life. With his new family, he moved into a new home, with the normal ups and downs of life. With his dedication to work, he received a promotion. He thought he had the respect of his workers, only to overhear them speak badly of him. He was discouraged by this and found it hard to cope.

♣ **Questions:** How can you keep your joy as a Christian in the midst of disharmony? Are you discouraged by what others say?

❖ **Read the Text**

Philippians 3:1–11
Christians should hold onto their joy in the midst of great sorrows and great trials of life, but they are easily discouraged by small things.

❖ **Search the Scriptures**

♣ **The dogs** (Philippians 3:1–2). The image of dogs was not positive in the scripture.

References: 1 Kings 14:11; Psalm 22:16–18; Matthew 15:26–28; Revelation 22:14–15

♣ **My identity** (Philippians 3:3–6). No confidence in human achievement.

References: Psalm 139:13–18; Matthew 16:13–10; 1 Corinthians 2:1–5

♣ **Knowing Christ** (Philippians 3:7–11). The most important thing is knowing Jesus Christ.

References: John 17:3; 1 John 5:20; 2 Peter 3:18

❖ **Closing**

LESSON 8

📖 **Joy in Faithfulness**

❖ **Opening**

❖ **Review**

❖ **Set the Tone**

♣ **Thought:** At the beginning of every year, many of us set goals. These may include the goal to grow more in Jesus Christ, to spend more time with family, to save more money, or to be healthier.

♣ **Questions:** Why do some people achieve their goals and others do not? How does one keep focused on the goals of life?

❖ **Read the Text**

Philippians 3:13–21
Paul calls the church to a different kind of faithfulness. He shares with the church that the way to experience God is through sticking with him.

❖ **Search the Scriptures**

♣ **Forget the past** (Philippians 3:12–14). Letting go of past achievements and successes is just as difficult as letting go of past pain and hurts.

References: Isaiah 43:18–19; Luke 9:61–62; 2 Corinthians 5:16–17

♣ **Spiritual maturity** (Philippians 3:15–16). The believer must strive to spiritually mature in Christ.

References: Luke 8:14–15; Hebrews 6:1–3; 1 Peter 2:2–3

♣ **Heavenly citizens** (Philippians 3:17–20). Our ultimate goal is to be citizens of heaven.

References: Hebrews 13:12–14; John 14:1–3; 1 Peter 1:3–4; Revelation 21:1–2

❖ **Closing**

LESSON 9

📖 Joy in Working with Others

❖ Opening

❖ Review

❖ Set the Tone

♣ **Thought:** A new independent church was started that was doing very well. It attracted both the unchurched and members from the traditional churches in the area. Those from the traditional churches boasted about their new experiences and new joys. About two years later, the pastoral team and the music team had a major disagreement, and the church had a split. The members were in a difficult position, and their faith was shaken.

♣ **Questions:** What do you do when there is disagreement in the church? How challenging is it to move on?

❖ Read the Text

Philippians 4:1–9
There is nothing that takes away the joy of serving the Lord like strained relationships in the church.

❖ Search the Scriptures

♣ **Settle disputes** (Philippians 4:1–5)

Settling disputes in the church—Euodia and Syntyche were probably deaconesses who worked alongside Paul. In Macedonia, women were permitted to be leaders. These two women had a quarrel.

References: Matthew 18:15–17; Ephesians 4:31–32; Romans 12:17–21; Colossians 3:12–15

♣ **Don't worry but pray** (Philippians 4:6–7). The more time you dedicate to prayer, the less time you spend worrying about the things you cannot control.

References: Matthew 6:25–34; 11:28–30; 1 Peter 5:6–8

♣ **Think and practice** (Philippians 4:8–10). The discipline of focusing your thoughts on excellent things will make a difference to you.

References: Romans 12:2; 2 Corinthians 10:5; 2 Timothy 1:7

❖ **Closing**

📖 **Joy in Giving**

❖ **Opening**

❖ **Review**

❖ **Set the Tone**

    ♣ **Thought:** Some churches are generous by nature. They take care of those in need, and they support missions.

    ♣ **Questions:** Is your church a giving church? Does your church give to missions?

❖ **Read the Text**

Philippians 4:10–23
Paul returns to the generosity of the Philippian church in these last few verses.

❖ **Search the Scriptures**

    ♣ **In times of need** (Philippians 4:10–14). The church was concerned about Paul's well-being.

    References: Luke 10:25–37; James 2:14–17

    ♣ **Financial blessings** (Philippians 4:15–17).

    References: Luke 6:38; Proverbs 3:9–10; 22:9; Malachi 3:10

❖ **Closing**

CHAPTER 5

The Christian Faith

📖 **Topic: The Christian Life**

❖ **Objective of Study:** The purpose of this series is to help new and experienced believers live a Christian life, according to the principles of the Word of God. For those who still doubt their faith, it is hoped that they will come to know with certainty that they have the gift of eternal life.

❖ **Duration: four lessons**

Lessons	Topic	Text
1	There Are Christians, and There Are Christians	John 3:1–8
2	The Diet Plan That Works for Christians	Philippians 1:1–6
3	Saved but Not Living Right	1 Thessalonians 4:1–12
4	When You Have Messed Up	Luke 22:54–62

LESSON 1

📖 **There Are Christians, and There Are Christians**

❖ **Opening**

❖ **Set The Tone**

♣ **Thought**: When I got my first job as a teacher, I usually got a ride to work with my aunt; that meant I got to work at least an hour and a half before school began. When I got to school, I would eat my breakfast, read my Bible, and pray before the students and most other teachers came.

One day, the music teacher came in to school early and saw me reading the Bible. He asked me what church I attended.

"The Moravian Church," I told him.

He immediately responded, "I thought you were a real Christian. Real Christians go to the Pentecostal Church, Church of God, Wesleyan, and so on."

But we in the Anglican, Methodist, or Moravian Church are churchgoers.

♣ **Questions:** What do you think about this comment? Do you think that thisC has changed today?

❖ **Read the Text**

John 3:1–8
In this text, Jesus explains the new experience of believers.

❖ **Search the Scripture**

Two references to the word *Christian* are found in Acts 11:25–26; 26:19–29; and 1 Peter 4:16.
The phrases more commonly used in the Bible were *disciples of Jesus Christ, followers of the way, brothers or sisters,* or *saints.*
Generally, Christians are followers of the teachings of Jesus Christ.
Today, there are three ways to think of the word *Christian*. There are Christians, and there are Christians.

♣ Christian, as a religion

Christianity is a major religion and the largest religion in the world, with 2.3 billion Christians. There are Christian nations, Christian countries, and Christian islands.

To be a Christian means that you identify more with Christianity than any of the other major religions. For example, on the island of Trinidad, someone might say, "I am a Christian," which means that I am not Muslim, Jew, or Hindu.

As Christians grew in number, they began to distinguish themselves from the Jews (Romans 9:1–5).

Today, however, to say that one is a Christian does not necessarily mean that one follows the teachings of Jesus Christ.

♣ Christian, as an upbringing

While 2.3 billion people consider themselves to be Christians, there are millions who have had a Christian upbringing. They have been nurtured in a Christian home with the practices, customs, sacraments, and rituals of Christianity. They attend church, regularly or occasionally. They are members of a particular Christian denomination—Roman Catholic, Episcopal, Moravian, Methodist, Pentecostal, Adventist—or nondenominational (2 Timothy 1:5; Ephesians 6:1–4).

♣ Christian, as a relationship

When Nicodemus came to Jesus, he was a member of the Jewish religion and had a solid Jewish upbringing. Jesus, however, introduced him to a new experience, which was relationship.

This relationship begins with the born-again or conversion experience. This goes beyond the covering of Christianity as a religion or the grace of the Christian upbringing.

It is about having a personal relationship with Jesus Christ (John 3:1–7).

It is confessing our sins, believing that Jesus died to change us, and accepting the gift of salvation (Romans 10:9–10; 1 John 1:8–10; Ephesians 2:8–9).

If you have taken this step, may you hold on and strengthen your faith. If you have not and desire to do so, let us pray the sinner's prayer.

Sinner's Prayer

Father in heaven, I know that I have sinned and that no amount of good works could ever make up for that. I believe that you love me and that you sent your Son, Jesus Christ, to die for me. Please forgive me of all my sins. Come into my heart and teach me how I should live. I offer you my life to use in whatever way you see fit. I trust that you know what is best for me. Change my whole life. I pray in Jesus's name, amen.

LESSON 2

📖 **Diet Plan That Works for Christians**

❖ **Opening**

❖ **Review Oof Lesson**

❖ **Set the Tone**

♣ **Thought:** The well-known Christian author Rick Warren has spoken of a new plan that he encouraged for his church. Due to concern for his own health, he recognized that he needed to do something about his life, and he started on the Daniel plan (Daniel 1:15). He encouraged members to do the same—to eat healthier, work out regularly, and join small groups. He lost sixty pounds.

♣ **Question:** Do you think that a pastor should be concerned about members' diets?

❖ **Read the Text**

Matthew 13:1–9, 18–23

The most important thing about any diet plan is not starting it but continuing it. Like our physical diet plan, we are required to maintain our diet so that we can prosper as Christians.

❖ **Search the Scriptures**

♣ **Gradual eating changes (Word of God)**

Milk (1 Peter 2:2–3).

Bread (Matthew 4:4; John 6:30–35—growing).

Meat/solid food (1 Corinthians 3:1–2; Hebrews 5:11–14; John 4:31–34—maturity).

♣ **Daily exercise routine (pray and seek God)**

Pray (Matthew 26:36–41; Philippians 4:6–7; Ephesians 6:18; James 5:13).

Seek God (Isaiah 55:6–7; 2 Chronicles 7:14).

♣ **Supplements (praise and worship)**

Worship (Psalm 43:11; 100; Hebrews 10:23–25).

Christian music (Colossians 3:16).

Christian books (Philippians 4; 8).

❖ **Closing**

--- LESSON 3 ---

📖 **Saved but Not Living Right**

❖ **Opening**

❖ **Review of Lessons**

❖ **Set the Tone**

♣ **Thought:** A pastor was approached by a disgruntled woman who complained that one of the members of the church was having a sexual relation with her boyfriend. The pastor said that he would investigate it but was convinced that it could not be the member he knew, who was saved. Upon inquiry, the member did not deny that it was true; she said that it was a weakness, especially because her husband was often away on military duties.

♣ **Question:** When you are not living right, does it mean that you are no longer saved?

❖ **Read the Text**

1 Thessalonians 4:1–12
It is a daily challenge to live a life that pleases God.

♣ **Sinful nature** (Galatians 5:19–21, 1 Thessalonians 4:3–5; Romans 8:5–8).

♣ **Breaking the bonds of sin** (Isaiah 58: 3–6; Mark 5:1–20).

♣ **Living in the Spirit** (Ephesians 4:20–24; 1 Peter 1:2, 1 Corinthians 6:11–20).

Closing

📖 **When You Have Messed Up**

❖ **Opening**

❖ **Review of Lessons**

❖ **Set the Tone**

♣ **Thought:** There were three cases in court recently in which the accused confessed that they deeply regretted their crimes: (1) the South African amputee track star who was accused of murdering his girlfriend; (2) two popular college students who were accused of raping a drunk girl; and (3) Jodi Arias, who was accused of stabbing her boyfriend. One common feature was that they all broke down into tears and cried almost uncontrollably.

♣ **Questions:** What does that say to you? Do tears usually mean that someone has done something? Does it mean the person is sorry? Does it mean that he or she will change?

❖ **Read the Text**

Luke 22:54–62
Messing up or failing, whether small or great, is something that happens to everyone. God's word teaches us that even when we mess up, he will not leave us but will lift us up.

❖ **Search the Scriptures**

♣ **Accept the failure**

Peter knew that he had failed everyone—Jesus, his fellow disciples, the followers of Jesus, and himself (Matthew 26:74–75; Joshua 7:1; 19–26; Psalm 51:3–4; Luke 15:18–19).

♣ **Time to reflect**

Peter experienced the wilderness as he returned to fishing. We can go into the wilderness experience (John 21:3; 1 Kings 19:3–4; Isaiah 59:1–2; Luke 15:13–17).

♣ **Restoration**

After that period of wilderness, God restores us to a higher place in him.

Peter was restored (Acts 2:1–4, 14–15; Luke 15:22–24; Joel 2:25).

❖ **Closing**

CHAPTER 6

Seven Deadly Sins

📖 Introduction of New Lesson

❖ Objective

To confront sin, which is destructive and can be deadly. To teach the believer that when sin is acknowledged, confessed, and forgiven that we position ourselves for God's peace in this present life and in eternal life.

❖ Duration of Study: eight lessons

Schedule

Lessons	Topic	Text
1	What Becomes of Sin?	Proverbs 6:16–19
2	Pride	Proverbs 16:14–19
3	Envy	Luke 22:24–30
4	Anger	Matthew 5:21–22
5	Sloth	Proverbs 6:1–6
6	Greed	Luke 18:18–30
7	Gluttony	1 Corinthians 6:9–20
8	Lust	2 Samuel 11:1–13

📖 **What Becomes of Sin?**

❖ **Opening**

❖ **Set the Tone**

    ♣ **Thought:** Using the word *sin* in public is like saying *bomb* on an airplane.

    ♣ **Questions:** Do you agree with this statement? Why or why not? What are some of the words that we are more comfortable with using?

❖ **Read the Text**

Proverbs 6:16–19

The seven deadly sins were so classified by the early church fathers who wanted the followers to stop certain behaviors that could destroy their lives. They believed that the sins could be replaced with Christian virtues.

❖ **Search the Scripture**

The most common Hebrew and Greek word for sin is *transgression*. This means to go outside or to step across the boundaries (1 John 3:4). It is like a sports player who goes outside the lines. The New Testament idea is from the Greek word *Harmatia*, which means missing the mark. It's like the sports player who does get the goal or hoop (Romans 6:20).

    ♣ **All have sinned**

        References: Romans 3:9–12; Isaiah 53:6; 1 John 1:8

    ♣ **Adamic sin**

        References: Psalm 51:5–6; Isaiah 64:6–7; Romans 5:12–21

♣ **The consequences of sin**

References: Genesis 2:16–17; Matthew 5:21–22; Romans 6:23

♣ **The answer for our sins**

References: Matthew 1:20–21; Psalm 103:8–12; 1 John 1:9

❖ **Closing**

📖 **Pride**

❖ **Opening**

❖ **Review of Lesson**

❖ **Set the Tone**

  ♣ **Thought**

> When I survey the wondrous cross
> On which the prince of glory died
> My richest gain I count but loss
> And pour contempt on all my pride

  ♣ **Question:** What does the above hymn mean?

❖ **Read the Text**

Proverbs 16:14–19
The Hebrew word for *pride* means to lift up or to be high.

❖ **Search the Scripture**

There is good pride and deadly pride.

  ♣ **Good**: Self-worth, self-esteem, self-confidence, desire to achieve

  ♣ **Deadly**: Arrogance, snobbery, haughtiness

  When we take our eyes from God and believe that we are responsible for who we are, that is deadly pride.

  ♣ **Stories of pride.**

  References: Power (Daniel 4:29–37); success (Luke 12:16–21); spirituality (Luke 18:9–14)

♣ **God opposes pride.**

References: James 4:6; Proverbs 16:18; 15:25

♣ **Christian virtue is humility.**

References: Luke 14:7–11; Philippians 2:3–4; James 4:7–10

❖ **Closing**

📖 **Envy**

❖ **Opening**

❖ **Review of Lessons**

❖ **Set the Tone**

♣ **Thought:** Surveys have shown that up to 60 percent of teens do not like who they are. They think that they are not good enough, as compared with other teens. Similarly, 40 percent of adults would rather be like someone else who is smarter, richer, better-looking, or more gifted(Pew research).

♣ **Question:** What do you think about these findings?

❖ **Read the Text**

Luke 22:24–30
Envy takes away the joy in our lives. It makes us feel like we are lacking something or that someone else is better than we are. It makes us feel bitter when others have it better.

❖ **Search the Scripture**

Envy is from the Hebrew word meaning jealousy and rivalry.

♣ **Stories of envy**

Sibling rivalry: Genesis 27:30–40; 37:2–8, 18–20
Neighbors' jealousy: Genesis 26:12–16, 1 Kings 21:1–16; Ecclesiastes 4:4

♣ **Spiritual envy**

Daniel 6:4; Luke 22:24–30; 1 Corinthians 12

♣ **Christian virtue**

James 3:14–18; Romans 12:6–8; Proverbs 14:30

❖ **Closing**

LESSON 4

📖 **Anger**

❖ **Opening**

❖ **Review of Lessons**

❖ **Set the Tone**

    ♣ **Thought:** An article in *Ebony* magazine suggested there are ten things that black people can learn from Barack Obama's life that will help them to be successful. The first one was learning to get over anger.

    The problem is not anger but "unresolved anger." You may have cooled down days, weeks, months, or years later, but that does not mean you have resolved the anger.

    ♣ **Question:** What causes people to get angry?

❖ **Read the Text**

Matthew 5:21–22
Anger is rated the number-one deadly sin. We are at our worst when we are angry.

❖ **Search the Scriptures**

Anger is an outburst of negative emotion, especially toward others.

    ♣ **Stories of anger**

    References: Genesis 4:1–10; Exodus 32:19–20; 1 Samuel 18:8–16

    ♣ **Dangers of anger**

    Proverbs 29:22; Psalm 4:4; Ephesians 4:26–27; James 1:19–20

    ♣ **Christian virtue**

    Proverbs 15:1; Psalm 37:8; Matthew 5:21–26

❖ **Closing**

LESSON 5

📖 **Sloth**

❖ **Opening**

❖ **Review of Lessons**

❖ **Set the Tone**

♣ **Thought:** Most food items today are available "ready to use." For example, peas are shelled, fish is scaled and cleaned, and rice is ready to cook. Some of the older folks think this is because we have a lazy generation who does not want to do the groundwork.

♣ **Questions:** Is this laziness? What is laziness?

❖ **Read the Text**

Proverbs 6:1–6
The word *sloth* is from the Greek word *akedeia*, which is a failure to make an effort, lack of care, indifference; it is more than laziness.

❖ **Search the Scriptures**

Slothfulness is a don't-care attitude

♣ **Stories of slothfulness**

References: Matthew 25:14–26, 2 Thessalonians 3:6–13; Proverbs 26:13–16

♣ **The consequences of laziness**

References: Proverbs 24:30–34; Ecclesiastes 10:18; Proverbs 21:25; 10:26

♣ **Christian virtue**

Work: Proverbs 6:6–11; Genesis 3:19; Hebrews 6:10–12

❖ **Closing**

LESSON 6

📖 **Greed**

❖ **Opening**

❖ **Review of Lessons**

❖ **Set the Tone**

　　♣ **Thought:** In 1923, the world's nine richest men gathered at a hotel in Chicago. Twenty-five years later, three were bankrupt and died penniless (including Charles Schwab), one went insane, two were imprisoned, and three committed suicide (www.forbes.com)

　　♣ **Question:** What do you believe is the reason for this?

❖ **Read the Text**

Luke 18:18–30
Greed is the word for covet and gain.

❖ **Search the Scriptures**

Greed is an excessive love of or desire for money or for any possession money can buy.

　　♣ **Stories of greed—mark of success**

　　　References: Luke 12:16–21; 15:11–19; Genesis 13:1–13

　　♣ **Dangers of greed**

　　　References: Proverbs 15:27; Jeremiah 6:12–13; Job 20:12–21; 1 Timothy 6:6–10

　　♣ **Christian virtue**

　　　References: Exodus 16:13–18; Matthew 6:25–34; Luke 12:32–34

Closing

📖 **Gluttony**

❖ **Opening**

❖ **Review of Last Lesson**

❖ **Set the Tone**

♣ **Thought:** One of the disciplines of the Black Muslims is that they eat only once a day. They do this because it is their belief that if they can control their appetites, they can control every other temptation.

♣ **Question:** Can you manage on one meal a day?

Gluttony is an uncontrolled desire to satisfy our imagined need for food.

❖ **Read the Text**

1 Corinthians 6:9–20
Gluttony is a sin that leads to physical destruction. Gluttony is to food as lust is to sex. It is the abuse and overindulgence that is the sin.

❖ **Search the Scriptures**

♣ **Stories of gluttony**

References: Numbers 11:18–34; Deuteronomy 21:18–20; Philippians 3:18–19

♣ **Jesus was accused of gluttony**

References: Luke 5:33; 7:33–34

♣ **God opposes gluttony**

References: Proverbs 23:2, 20–21; 1 Corinthians 10:7; Titus 1:12

♣ **Christian virtue**

Spiritual focus: 1 Timothy 6:6–8; Matthew 5:6

Closing

LESSON 8

📖 **Lust**

❖ **Opening**

❖ **Review of Last Lessons**

❖ **Set the Tone**

   ♣ **Thought:** "Beware of lust; it corrupts both the body and the mind" (Zoroaster).

   ♣ **Question:** What do you think of the above quote?

❖ **Read the Text**

2 Samuel 11:1–13

The word *lust* in biblical terms means passionate desire (especially sexual desire) or desire for worldly pleasures. Lust is associated with passion that stirs up sexual emotion.

❖ **Search the Scriptures**

   ♣ **Stories of lust**: 2 Samuel 13:1–15; Matthew 5:28; Romans 1:24

   ♣ **The consequences of lust**: Proverbs 6:25–26; James 1:14–15; 2 Peter 2:9–10

   ♣ **Christian virtues**: Colossians 3:5; 1 Thessalonians 4:4–5; 2 Timothy 2:22

❖ **Closing**

CHAPTER 7

Worshipping Christ or Celebrating Customs

📖 Objective

To give a better understanding of the customs and practices of the Moravian Church and how we can worship God through them and grow in our faith in Jesus Christ. Why do we do what we do?

❖ Duration of Study: four lessons

❖ Schedule

Lessons	Topic	Text
1	The Sacraments	1 Corinthians 10:16–22
2	The Rites	Acts 8:9–17
3	Moravian Memorial Dates	Deuteronomy 11:16–21
4	Love Feast/Cup of Covenant	Nehemiah 1:1–11

📖 **The Sacraments**

❖ **Opening**

❖ **Introduction of Lesson**

❖ **Set the Tone**

♣ **Thought:** I met a young lady who informed me that she was a member of the Moravian Church. Her mother, an elder, reminded her to pay her tithes weekly and to take Holy Communion three times a year so that she could remain an active communicant member. This young lady then said, "I did one Communion already for the year, and I have two more to go."

♣ **Questions:** Should Moravians think about Communion only three times a year? How important is Holy Communion to believers?

❖ **Read the Text**

1 Corinthians 10:16–22

A sacrament is a religious ceremony that Christians believe is a visible sign of the grace of God. Sacraments mark or seal the believers.

❖ **Search the Scriptures**

♣ **Understanding sacraments**

There are two sacraments in the Moravian Church: baptism and Holy Communion.

Roman Catholics observe seven sacraments: baptism, confirmation, Eucharist (Communion), penance, anointing of the sick, matrimony, and holy order.

Most of the Reformed or Protestant churches have two: baptism and Holy Communion.

The Anglican (Episcopalian) and the Methodist churches believe that two sacraments are ordained by Jesus Christ, and the other five are not sacraments of the gospel.

Baptists and Pentecostals don't use the word *sacraments*; rather, they use *ordinance* because they think that sacraments give too much power to the priest or pastor.

The Salvation Army and Quakers have no sacraments, although their members can go to other churches to partake in the sacraments.

2 Thessalonians 2:15

♣ **Baptism: We believe in baptism**

Command from Jesus: Matthew 28:19–20

Makes us one: Ephesians 4:3–6

Is extended to all: Acts 16:25–34, 1 Corinthians 1:10–17; 12:13

Public testimony of salvation: Mark 1: 4–5; 16:15–16; Acts 2:38–41

♣ **Holy Communion**

Command from Jesus: Matthew 26:26–28

Memorial of Christ: 1 Corinthians 11:17–26; John 6:53–58

Christian fellowship: Acts 2:42–46; 20:7

Personal examination: 1 Corinthians 11:26–34

The sacraments must be rooted in a relationship with Christ. Then they strengthen the faith of the believers.

1 Corinthians 11:2

❖ **Closing**

📖 **The Rites**

❖ **Opening**

❖ **Review of Lesson**

❖ **Set the Tone**

   ♣ **Thought:** A young pastor was trying to start a confirmation class, only to realize that no one was interested. When he spoke to one of the youths, she said, "I was told that it's memorizing verses, and it won't get me into the kingdom of God." The pastor explained to her that it was instruction in the Word of God. She joined and is today an elder and a lay preacher, and she encourages young people to affirm their faith.

   ♣ **Questions:** Is confirmation seen as a positive or negative practice?

Read the Text

   Acts 8:9–17
   A *rite* is a religious ceremony or act in the church, through which a status or privilege is granted.
   There are three rites in the Moravian Church: confirmation, marriage, and ordination.
   Confirmation—membership
   Marriage—married
   Ordination—clergy

   Confirmation:

❖ **Search the Scripture**

   ♣ **Confirmation**. The word *confirmation* is not in the Bible, but we see it as a time of teaching, in preparation for affirming one's faith in Jesus Christ and confirming the sacrament of baptism, if done in infancy.

   References: Instruction (Luke 2:41–47); testimony/hope (Matthew 10:32); laying on of hands (Acts 8:14–17)

♣ **Marriage.** The Moravian Church acknowledges that marriage is between one male and one female. It is the official joining after careful preparation.

References: Genesis 1:27–28; blessed by Jesus (John 2:1–12; Matthew 19:6); sacred relationships (Hebrews 13:4; Ephesians 5:21–33)

♣ **Ordination:** Setting aside of men and women for focus on ministry.

References: Exodus 28:41; John 21: 15–17; Ephesians 4:11–12

❖ **Closing**

📖 **Moravian Memorial Dates**

❖ **Opening**

❖ **Review of Last Lesson**

❖ **Set the Tone**

    ♣ **Thought:** There are special dates on the calendar to remember special events, from New Year's to Valentine's Day to birthdays, anniversaries, and Christmas.

    ♣ **Question:** What is the point of special dates?

❖ **Read the Text**

Ecclesiastes 3:1–8
The church year begins with Advent and ends with the Pentecost season.

❖ **Search the Scripture**

As a liturgical church, we celebrate the seasons. It is a great time for the church to live the whole life of Jesus Christ and remind ourselves of what he has done for us, is doing now, and promises to do for the future.

    Advent (Matthew 1:23; Matthew 25:31–33)
    Christmas (Luke 1:26–33)
    Epiphany (Matthew 2:7–12)
    Lent (Matthew 4:1–3)
    Palm Sunday (Mark 11:1–11)
    Good Friday (Mark 15:33–47)
    Easter (Mark 16:1–8)
    Ascension (Acts 1:6–11)
    Pentecost (Acts 2:1–13)
    Trinity Sunday (John 1:1–14)

❖ **Closing**

📖 **Love Feasts/Cup of Covenant**

❖ **Opening**

❖ **Review of Last Lesson**

❖ **Set the Tone**

   ♣ **Thought:** All churches have their various celebrations. These are the dates that are used to commemorate a significant event. As a Moravian church, we have many dates, but we choose annually to celebrate some significant ones.

   ♣ **Question:** What is your favorite Moravian celebration?

Read the Text

Deuteronomy 11:16–21
Memorial dates are for remembrance and celebration.

❖ **Search the Scripture**

March 1 (1457)—Founding of the unity (John 17:20–26)
March 26 (1467)—Beginning of ordained ministry (Mark 1:16–20)
May 12 (1727)—Signing of brotherly agreement (Romans 3:27–31)
July 6 (1415)—Martyrdom of John Huss (Revelation 7:13–17)
August 13 (1732)—Outpouring of the Spirit (Acts 2:1–5)
August 21 (1732)—Date of first missionaries from Herrnhut (Matthew 28:16–20)
September 16—Minister's Covenant Day (John 17:13–19)
November 13 (1741)—Jesus Christ as chief elder (Ephesians 5:23–24)
December 13 (1732)—Arrival of first missionaries (Acts 4:4–8)

   ♣ **Love feasts**. This was started in 1727 to keep fellowship together among believers who were excited to talk about the teachings of Jesus Christ. The Moravian love feasts are today celebrated primarily at anniversaries and missionary services (Acts 2:46).

♣ **Cup of covenant**. This was used as a sign of renewed commitment to service. Believers came together to thank God for his mercies and to unite in faithfulness in the work of the Lord. It was only celebrated among officers and leaders of the church (Luke 22:17).

❖ **Closing**

CHAPTER 8

The Bible in Today's World

📖 **Pushing Past Life's Setbacks and Disappointments**

❖ Opening

❖ Introduction of New Lesson

❖ Objective

To encourage every believer to trust God fully in the midst of their struggles and challenges. It is a reminder of Proverbs 3:6—"Trust in the Lord with all thine heart and lean not unto thine own understanding but in all thy ways acknowledge him and he shall direct thy paths."

Lessons	Topic	Text
1	Sickness/Healing	Matthew 8:5–17
2	Loss of Loved Ones	Genesis 48:1–22
3	Financial Loss/Bankruptcy	Joel 2:25–27
4	Separation/Divorce	Matthew 19:1–6
5	Prodigal Children	Luke 15:11–32
6	Failure/Lack of Motivation	Psalm 42:1–11

LESSON 1

📖 Sickness/Healing

❖ Opening

❖ Review of Lesson

❖ Set the Tone

 ♣ **Thought:** A very close relative was diagnosed with stage 4 cancer and died within a few months. She was forty-seven years old. This was a shock for everyone because she had been a very active woman, like the women of Proverbs 31. She used her many gifts and skills at home, work, and in ministry in the church.

 ♣ **Question:** How does a family, church, and community see God in the midst of the above situation?

❖ Read the Text

Matthew 8:5–17
Healing of all manner of diseases was central to the ministry of Jesus.

❖ Search the Scripture

Sickness is not easy. When a close relative or loved is ill or if it's your own sickness, it can take its toll on you, physically, emotionally, and spiritually. But God is there in the midst of all sickness.

 ♣ **Illness is no respecter of persons.** We noted that the young servant was paralyzed and in pain. In the Bible, people were struck with many illnesses.

 References: Royalty (1 Kings 14:1–11); accidents (2 Kings 1:2–5); servants of God (Philippians 2:25–27)

♣ **Sickness humbles us.** It teaches us a lesson. It strips our pride from us. It can be a blessing in disguise. If the servant had not been sick, the officer would not have met Jesus.

References: Paul (2 Corinthians 12:7–10); Job (Job 2:4–10); Hezekiah (Isaiah 38:15–20)

♣ **It increases our faith.** When we are sick, we ask God to heal us. We pray more. We read his Word more. We trust him more. We need faith to believe in divine healing.

References: Matthew 17:14–18; Luke 17: 11–19; James 5: 13–15

♣ **Pray for the healing of the soul**. While physical healing is needed, we pray more so for the healing of the soul (James 5:16; 2 Corinthians 4:16–18; 3 John 1:2).

❖ **Closing**

LESSON 2

📖 **Loss of Loved Ones**

❖ **Opening**

❖ **Review of Lesson**

❖ **Set the Tone**

   ♣ **Thought**

> Grieve not for me though I am gone
> For I am with you still.
> God grant you strength to carry on
> And understand His will.
> A soft tear shed from time to time
> Will ease your sorrowed mind,
> But live your life as fully
> As you helped me live mine.
> Time will heal the hurting heart,
> Faith will see you through.
> There's still a life left for you to live,
> With courage I leave you.
> Remember me with thoughts of peace,
> Live each day with your heart;
> Grieve not for me though I am gone,
> We're never far apart. (Patricia Ann Boyes, www.paboyes.com)

   ♣ **Questions:** What thoughts come to your mind as you read this poem? Do you think that we take these words seriously?

❖ **Read the Text**

Genesis 48:1–22.

Loss brings indescribable pain and sadness. God is the only one who brings us hope, peace, and joy in the midst of our loss.

❖ **Search the Scripture**

♣ **Grief is very personal**. No two people will respond in the same way to loss. Consider Job's and David's responses to the deaths of their respective children (Job 3:11–13; 2 Samuel 12:15–23)

Stages of grief:
> Denial—sudden
> Anger—that the person left them
> Guilt—could I have done more?
> Sadness/depression—pain and is the longest stage
> Acceptance—it happened; funeral service

♣ **God cares about our grief**.

Does Jesus care when I've said goodbye
To the dearest on earth to me,
And my sad heart aches till it nearly breaks
Is it aught to him? Does He see?
O yes, He cares, I know He cares,
His heart is touched with my grief.
When the days are weary, the long nights dreary,
I know my Savior cares. (The Isaacs)

References: Isaiah 53:4; Psalm 46:1–7; John 11:17–37; 2 Corinthians 1:3–4; Matthew 5:4

♣ **Help is needed**. Christians should not grieve alone. We should get support from fellow believers and seek professional help.

References: Romans 12:15; Galatians 6:2–3; John 19:26–27

♣ **Do not lose hope**. We will have hope for those who died in Christ. And for those we are not sure of, we trust that they would have made a decision for Christ.

References: Lamentations 3:19–24; 1 Thessalonians 4:13–14; Philippians 1:20–21; Revelation 21:1–4; (Hope for unsaved) Luke 23: 39–43

♣ **Commemorate and celebrate.** Creating a memorial of some sort helps in healing, but the most important memorial is a spiritual one. What is God calling me to do during my grief?

References: Joshua 4:4–7; (God's call) Isaiah 6:1–8

❖ **Closing**

LESSON 3

📖 **Prodigal Children**

❖ **Opening**

❖ **Review of Lessons**

❖ **Set the Tone**

♣ **Thought:** A local newspaper had the story of a famous boxer from a famous boxing family who was arrested and charged with statutory rape—he was accused of having sexual relations with a fifteen-year-old girl. According to the article, he knew her age but still had sexual relations with her several times. This is a sad and heartbreaking story, but it is even more difficult because this is also a well-known Christian family. It is family that has reached out to at-risk youth and has guided them away from a life of crime and violence.

♣ **Questions:** How do you think that family is feeling now? What advice would you give to the father?

❖ **Read the Text**

Luke 15:11–32
Even in Christian families, children do go astray. How do we, as believers, deal with prodigal children?

❖ **Search the Scripture**

♣ **Children make their own decisions.** As much as we would like to choose for our children, we must accept that they make their own choices.

References: Commandment (Ephesians 6:1–3); responsibilities (John 9:17–21); Choices (Jeremiah 31:29–30); Proverbs 20:11

♣ **Parents should do what they can when they can.**

References: (Train) Deuteronomy 11:18–21; Proverbs 22:6; (Discipline) Ephesians 6:4; Proverbs 23:13–14

♣ **Parents should be loving and compassionate**. Love and compassion were not practiced in the Old Testament (Deuteronomy 21:18–21). Just like the Father, parents must have unconditional love (Luke 15: 20; Psalm 103:13–14; Isaiah 49:15; Ephesians 4:32).

♣ **It's for the prodigal child that Jesus has died**. God cares for all. He sent his Son to bring back those who have strayed.

References: Luke 15:25–32; Jeremiah 31:16–17; Lamentations 3:31–33; Matthew 18:12–13

❖ **Closing**

LESSON 4

📖 **Failure/Discouragement**

❖ **Opening**

❖ **Review of Lesson**

❖ **Set the Tone**

♣ **Thought:** After his divorce, a leader of the church withdrew from the public eye and stopped attending church. When visited by the pastor, he said that he was too ashamed to face anyone, for he felt like a total failure: "I failed my family. I failed my church. I failed my friends. I failed myself, and I failed God."

♣ **Questions:** Have you ever felt like a failure? Can we fail God?

❖ **Read the Text**

Psalm 42:1–11
How do we deal with seasons of discouragement after failure?

❖ **Search the Scripture**

Types of failures

♣ **Common/daily**—Forgetting an appointment that was important; losing a game; missing a deadline (filing taxes)

♣ **Professional**—Failing at your job/career

♣ **Business**—Suffering major financial loss

♣ **Family failure**—Strained family relations; separation; divorce

♣ **Morality**—Inappropriate relationships; mishandling of funds; criminal activity

♣ **Failure is humbling**.

References: Jonah 1:1–12; Daniel 4:4–5, 27–37

♣ **Failure is temporary for the godly.**

References: Psalm 37:23–25; Proverbs 24:16; Micah 7:7–10; 1 Corinthians 10:12–13

♣ **Forgiveness is key.**

References: (Seek forgiveness) Luke 15:2; Psalm 52:14; (receive God's forgiveness) Psalm 103:10–14; Isaiah 1:18

♣ **Encourage yourself.**

References: 1 Samuel 30:6; Psalm 40:1–5; Philippians 3:12–14

❖ **Closing**

CHAPTER 9

Jehovah Jireh, Our Provider

📖 **Introduction of New Lesson**

❖ **Objective:** To instruct us on biblical ways to be better stewards of God's money so that we can be victors and not victims of our finances.

❖ **Duration:** six lessons

❖ **Schedule of Study**

Lessons	Topic	Text
1	Developing the Right Attitude	Matthew 6:24–34
2	Earning a Living	2 Thessalonians 3:6–11
3	Savings and Investing	Matthew 25:14–30
4	Borrowing and Lending	Deuteronomy 28:8–14
5	God's Way of Receiving	Philippians 4:10–19
6	Leaving an Inheritance	Proverbs 13:20–25

📖 **Developing the Right Attitude**

❖ **Opening**

❖ **Review**

❖ **Set the Tone**

    ♣ **Thought:** I had the privilege of chaperoning a group of high school students to New York to attend a model UN conference. In my assigned group, it was interesting to observe the differences in their approach to money.

    One student was from a well-off family, yet she was very careful about every cent that she spent. She was interested only in the cheapest meals and had no interest in spending on anything else. Every evening, she called her dad and gave him an account of the money she'd spent and how much she left. At times, it was stressful to the other members, who would prefer to splurge a little. But she was always of the belief that she was not going to spend more than twenty dollars a day for breakfast, lunch, and dinner.

    ♣ **Questions:** Is this the right attitude toward money? Should we be taken up with every cent? Should we be free to spend?

❖ **Read the Text**

Matthew 6:24–34

    ♣ **Unchristian attitudes toward money**

    Fear: 1 Kings 17:8–14; Matthew 6:25–34
    Love: Ecclesiastes 5:10; Luke 16:13–15; Hebrews 13:5; 1 Timothy 6:10
    Carelessness: Deuteronomy 8:11–17; Luke 15:11–14; 16:1–2, 11–12

    ♣ **Christian attitudes toward money**

    Thankful: Philippians 4:10–13; 1 Timothy 6:6–8
    Trustful: Philippians 4:18–20; Psalm 37:25; Proverbs 3:5–6
    Careful: Deuteronomy 8:18–20; Mark 8:36

❖ **Closing**

LESSON 2

📖 **Earning a Living**

❖ **Opening**

❖ **Review of Lesson**

❖ **Set the Tone**

♣ **Thought:** In a particular charismatic group, some members refused to work because they claimed that they were dedicating themselves to praying, fasting, and evangelizing. The other members of the group worked and took care of them. One of the workers was not pleased and said that the group of believers were lazy and were home sleeping and watching TV, while the others did the work of the Lord.

♣ **Questions:** Do believers use ministry as an excuse not to work? Should every believer earn a living?

❖ **Read the Text**

2 Thessalonians 3:6–11
When God says that he will provide, what does that mean?

❖ **Search the Scripture**

♣ **God created us to work.**

References: Genesis 2:4–15; 3:17–19; Nehemiah 4:6; 1 Thessalonians 4:9–12

♣ **Have a Christlike approach to work.**

References: Matthew 20:1–15; 2 Thessalonians 3:6–10; Matthew 9:35–28; 2 Timothy 2:6

♣ **Work fulfills God's purpose for us.**

Personal fulfilment: Galatians 6:4–10; Ecclesiastes 5:18–20; Colossians 3: 23–24

❖ **Closing**

📖 **Savings and Investing**

❖ **Opening**

❖ **Review of Lesson**

❖ **Set the Tone**

    ♣ **Thought:** There was a Christian couple who worked for five years and saved one of their salaries. When they had their children, the wife chose to reduce her work hours so that she could spend more time at home because they had saved enough money to live on.

    ♣ **Questions:** Does the average couple save for children? What do we save for?

❖ **Read the Text**

Matthew 25:14–30
Part of our stewardship as Christians is saving and investing.

❖ **Search the Scripture**

Savings is different from investments. Savings is earning interest and returns without putting your original contribution at risk. Investing is risking the original for a greater return.

    ♣ **Saving is wise.**

Mathew 25:27; Proverbs 6:6–8; 21:20

Practical ways of saving are through the bank, credit union, insurance companies.

♣ **Investment is risky but necessary.**

References: Proverbs 21:5; 24:27; Luke 14:28–30; Ecclesiastes 5:13–15; Matthew 25:14–30

♣ **Have a retirement plan.**

Proverbs 27:12; Numbers 8: 23–26; Psalm 71:16–19; Galatians 6:9

❖ **Closing**

📖 **Borrowing and Lending**

❖ **Opening**

❖ **Review of Lessons**

❖ **Set the Tone**

♣ **Thought:** There are many Christian seminars on how to become debt-free. There are many testimonies of Christians who were able to get out of debt. I have heard of members who are living debt-free lives.

♣ **Questions:** Is it possible to live without borrowing? Can you get a house or car or complete your studies or your children's studies without borrowing?

❖ **Read the Text**

Deuteronomy 28:8–14
The Bible is clear that God expects the godly to be lenders and not borrowers.

❖ **Search the Scripture**

♣ **Borrowing**

Necessary: 2 Kings 4:1–7; Luke 10:33–35; Nehemiah 5:1–7
Obligations: Proverbs 22:7; 11:15; 22:26–27; Exodus 22:14

♣ **Lending**

Blessed lender: Deuteronomy 28:11–14; Psalm 37:26; 112:5
Godly lending: Leviticus 25:35–36; Deuteronomy 15:7–11; 23:19–20; Proverbs 28:8; 3:27–28; Matthew 5:42

♣ **Repaying**

Psalm 37:21; Matthew 18: 23–35; Romans 13: 6–7

❖ **Closing**

LESSON 5

📖 **God's Way of Receiving**

❖ **Opening**

❖ **Review of Lesson**

❖ **Set the Tone**

   ♣ **Thought**: A pastor of a church testified of the blessings of the Lord—the church received, from an anonymous donor, the lump sum of $200,000. It was later discovered that the money came from a member who had won the lottery.

   ♣ **Questions:** Is this a blessing from God? Or should the pastor give back the money?

❖ **Read the Text**

Philippians 4:10–19
God has promised to provide for us, but are all the ways the right ways?
Christians are not to rely on:

   ♣ **Gambling.** It is deceptive and destructive.

     References: Proverbs 28:19–20; 13:11; Zechariah 7:9–10

   ♣ **Public assistance only.** We all need help from time to time but should not be dependent on a system.

     References: James 2:14–16; 2 Thessalonians 3:9–13; Psalm 37:25

   Christians receive from God by:
      Asking.
      References: 1 John 3:21–22; Mark 11:24; Matthew 7:7–11; John 16:24
      Giving.
      References: 2 Corinthians 9:6–10; Luke 6:38; Malachi 3:9–12

❖ **Closing**

📖 **Leaving an Inheritance**

❖ **Opening**

❖ **Review Lesson**

❖ **Set the Tone**

♣ **Thought:** There was a series on the OWN network titled *The Will: Family Secrets Revealed*. In these shows, a person with fame or money has died and left an inheritance. However, as the estate is about to be distributed, other family members turn up to share—children who were not known, ex-wives, ex-husbands, etc. What I have noticed is that there are long legal battles and, in the end, it seems that nobody really wins.

♣ **Question:** Why is estate sharing usually a battle?

❖ **Read the Text**

Proverbs 13:20–25
Part of the good stewardship of Christians is to ensure that we can pass on—not just to one generation but to the following generations—what the Lord has blessed us with.

Search the Scripture

♣ **Inheritance for children**

Proverbs 13:22

Sons: Proverbs 19:14; Ezekiel 46:16–18; Deuteronomy 21:15–17; 2 Chronicles 21:2–4

Daughters protested: Numbers 27:1–11; Job 42:15

♣ **Right timing**

Proverbs 20:21; Luke 15:12–19; (will and living trust) Hebrews 9:16–17

♣ **Godly inheritance**

Luke 12: 13–21; Colossians 1:11,12; 1 Peter 1:3–4

Closing

CHAPTER 10

Sexual Relationships: The Christian Approach

📖 **Introduction of New Lesson**

❖ **Objective:** To guide Christian believers to a biblical and nonjudgmental approach to some of their and their loved ones' struggles around the complex issue of human sexuality and romantic relationships

Text: Proverbs 21:2. People may be right in their own eyes, but God examines their hearts.

Duration: four lessons

Schedule

Lessons	Topic	Text
1	God's Plan for Sexuality	Genesis 2:18–25
2	Is Sexual Purity Possible?	1 Thessalonians 4:1–8
3	LGBT: A Christian Approach	Genesis 18:16–33
4	Common Law Union: A Christian Approach	Genesis 24:52–67

GOD'S PLAN FOR SEXUALITY

❖ **Opening**

❖ **Review**

❖ **Set the Tone**

♣ **Thought:** The church has its head buried in the ground when it come to sexuality. Like parents of older generations, the church would prefer not to talk about it, in the hope they will not have to answer uncomfortable and difficult questions.

♣ **Question:** Do you agree that the church is afraid to talk about sexuality?

❖ **Read the Text**

Genesis 2:18–25
Sexuality has changed with time. It is generally defined as the way people experience and express themselves sexually. It is about feelings, thoughts, behavior, and attraction.

❖ **Search the Scriptures**

Sexuality is a gift from God to humans. God created us as sexual creatures. That is why he created relationship from the beginning:

♣ **Created as sexual creatures:** Genesis 2:18–25; Song of Solomon 7:6–12

♣ **Purpose for sexual expression**

Procreation: Genesis 1:28; 4:1–2; Malachi 2:15

Union: Genesis 2:24; Matthew 19:4–6; Ephesians 5:28–29

Pleasure: 1 Corinthians 7:2–5; Song of Solomon 5:16; Proverbs 5:18–19; Genesis 26:8–11

♣ **Purpose for celibacy**

1 Corinthians 7:32–35; Matthew 19:11–12

❖ **Closing**

LESSON 2

📖 **Is Sexual Purity Possible?**

❖ **Opening**

❖ **Review of Lesson**

❖ **Set the Tone**

♣ **Thought:** A few years ago, Russell Wilson, the famous quarterback for the Seattle Seahawks, shared a video in which he said that he was planning to abstain from a sexual relationship with his girlfriend until they got married. He said that he and his girlfriend had decided to do it Jesus's way.

Wilson's fellow athletes and his fans were shocked at this revelation. They didn't think that it was possible or necessary.

♣ **Question:** Do you think it is possible?

❖ **Read the Text**

1 Thessalonians 4:1–8
Christian believers were taught that sexual relations were to be only in the context of marriage. Any sexual relation outside of marriage was impure.

❖ **Search the Scriptures**

In spite of what may have been cultural norms, Paul calls believers to sexually pure living.

♣ **A call to holy living** (1 Thessalonians 4:3): To be holy is to be set apart. It is to be different. The way of the believer is through holy living (Job 4:17–19; 1 Peter 1:13–16; 1 Corinthians 1:2–3; Genesis 39:6–12).

♣ **Control of the body** (1 Thessalonians 4:4): One of the fundamental Montessori education principles is to learn to control your body. If you can control your body, then you can control how you live. This is an important Christian principle as well (1 Corinthians 6:12–20; 2 Samuel 11:2–5; Romans 6:11–14).

♣ **Temporal and eternal consequences of lack of self-control:** 1 Thessalonians 4:8; Proverbs 5:1–14; Judges 16:4–22; 1 Corinthians 6: 9–11

❖ **Closing**

LESSON 3

📖 **7LGBT: A Christian Approach**

❖ **Opening**

❖ **Review of Lesson**

❖ **Set the Tone**

♣ **Thought:** One of the Democratic presidential candidates for the 2020 election -was Pete Buttigieg. Mr. Buttigieg and then–Vice President Mike Pence got into an argument over the rights of gays. Mr. Buttigieg is openly gay and told Pence, "If you have problem with my gayness, take it up with God … If you have a problem with who I am, your problem is not with me. Your quarrel, sir, is with my Creator."

♣ **Questions:** What do you understand by Mr. Buttigieg's statements? Do you agree with him?

❖ **Read the Text**

Genesis 18:16–33
The most commonly held view is that the sin of Sodom and Gomorrah is homosexuality. It is also believed that the real sin was that the cities were inhospitable to strangers.

❖ **Search the Scriptures**

Understanding LGBTQ
Lesbian: a woman who is only or almost only sexually attracted to women
Gay: a man who is only or almost only sexually attracted to men
Bisexual: a male or female who is equally attracted to both genders
Transgender: a male or female who does not identify with his or her birth sex.
Questioning/queer: a person who does not conform with either male or female norms

♣ **All created by God** (Psalm 139:13–16; Job 10:8–12; Malachi 2:10; Genesis 5:2; Mark 10:6; Psalm 51:5).

♣ **Condemnation or compassion**. LGBTQ are already in a struggle with God about their feelings and attraction. Further condemnation from believers will not help.

References: Matthew 9:35–38; Psalm 119:49–52; Proverbs 16:23–24; Titus 3:1–2

♣ **Our prayer should be for a committed relationship with Christ** (Isaiah 56:3–8; John 4:13–24; 2 Timothy 1:8–12).

❖ **Closing**

LESSON 4

📖 **Common Law Union: A Christian Approach**

❖ **Opening**

❖ **Review of Lessons**

❖ **Set the Tone**

The church board of a congregation had eight members, with some seven faithful sisters in Christ and one senior male. The new pastor was working with the board to find new ways to move forward and to grow the church. The board was of the view that one of the prominent members, who held most of the leadership positions, was keeping the church back. The pastor was encouraged to do something about it.

Soon after the meeting, the pastor of the church was confronted by the daughter of the prominent member. The daughter informed the pastor and the church that the women on the board did not like her mother because unlike them, who were living with men but not married, her mother had been married for more than fifty years.

The pastor discovered the daughter's claim was true—most of the women on the church board were living in common law unions.

♣ **Questions:** How common is living together? How is it looked upon? Is it acceptable to God?

❖ **Read the Text**

Genesis 24:52–67

❖ **Search the Scriptures**

A common law union is a relationship between two persons in which they reside together for an extended time without a formal ceremony. The union generally involves sexual activity, offspring, shared household duties, and shared financial responsibilities.

Marriage is a formal union and a social and legal contract between two individuals that unites their lives. It similarly generally involves sexual activity, offspring, shared household duties, and shared financial responsibilities.

Christian marriage counselors say that the reasons for the common law union in the church are as follows:

Many find themselves in the position before they had a commitment to Christ.

It is a family norm—one's great-grandmother or grandmother did it; one's mother did it, etc.

Fear of ruining the relationship—a good "live with" is better than a bad marriage.

Legal benefits—why bother to commit?

Practical—it's an economic issue.

The Bible is favorable toward marriage.

Marriage is instituted by God (Genesis 2:21–25; 29:9–30; Hebrews 13:4).

Marriage is likened to divine relationship (Isaiah 62:4–5; Ephesians 5:21–33; Revelation 19:7–9).

Marriage union is blessed by God (Genesis 1:27–28; John 2:1–12; Proverbs 18:22).

❖ Closing

ACKNOWLEDGMENTS

I have been taught as much as I have taught during Bible studies over the years. Therefore, I wish to thank all the members and those who have attended Bible studies for their input, presence, and encouragement.

A special thanks to Sister Jeanette Smith-Barry and Sister Mary L. Harley for their faithfulness in editing this work for me. Also, my heartfelt thanks to Sister Carla Smith-Todman for typesetting and to Desiree Gumbs for the book cover design; to my mother for her words of encouragement during the process; and to my husband, Mikie, and our daughters, Tsedek, Tsamara, and Tsalom. I am appreciative of your continued support.

Above all, I give God thanks and praise for his all-sufficient grace and sustaining mercy.

ABOUT THE AUTHOR

Bible study has been the central focus and passion of Winelle Kirton-Roberts during her twenty-six years of ordained ministry in the Moravian Church. As a gifted teacher, she has served as pastor of Moravian churches in Trinidad, Barbados, and St. Thomas, Virgin Islands, and she currently pastors a new Moravian fellowship in Geneva, Switzerland. In addition to pastoral ministry, she has held administrative positions, including secretary of the Provincial Elders Conference (2015–19) and superintendent of the Virgin Islands Conference (2009–14).

Dr. Kirton-Roberts holds a PhD in church history. Her first book, *Created in Their Image*, was published in 2015, followed by entries in the *Encyclopedia of Christianity in the Global South*. She has given several public lectures in history, including the Moses lecture for Moravian University in Bethlehem, Pennsylvania, and as a keynote speaker for Wake Forest University, Winston-Salem, North Carolina.

She is married to Mikie Roberts, and they have three daughters.